NOTES BELOW THE STAFF

NOTES BELOW THE STAFF

A MEMOIR

HERBERT BEATTIE
WITH LAUREN ARNEST

East of the Mountains  and West of the Sun

RHYOLITE PRESS LLC
Colorado Springs, Colorado

Ccopyright © 2019 Herbert Beattie

All Rights Reserved. No portion of this book may be reproduced in any form or by any electronic or mechanical means, including information storage and retrieval systems, without permission from the publisher, except by a reviewer who may quote brief passages in a review. Every reasonable attempt has been made to identify owners of copyright. Errors or omissions will be corrected in subsequent editions.

❑

Published in the United States of America
by Rhyolite Press, LLC
P.O. Box 60144
Colorado Springs, Colorado 80960
www.rhyolitepress.com

Beattie, Herbert
with Lauren Arnest

NOTES BELOW THE STAFF

1st edition: July, 2019

Library of Congress Control Number: 2019946042
ISBN 978-1-943829-22-4

❐

PRINTED IN THE UNITED STATES OF AMERICA

Cover design, book design/layout
by Donald R. Kallaus

For Laurie

CONTENTS

Foreword ix

THE LIFE

The Packing: Ye Gods! 1
The Traveling: Prepare to Die 2
The Lodging: Are Those Bed Bugs? 4
The Food: Did the Laundry Shrink My Pants? 6
The Payoff: Why Am I Here? 7

THE CONDUCTORS

Josef Krips: "Ze *Fly*?" 11
Peter Herman Adler: "You've Got to Be Kidding!" 13
William Steinberg: Te Deum or Tedium 16
Eugene Ormandy: Thus Saith the . . . Conductor 18
Pablo Casals: Oxygen 21
John Finley Williamson: The Disappearing Conductor 25
Sarah Caldwell: What Will Happen Next? 28
Kurt Herbert Adler: Charming! 30
Emerson Buckley: Buck 32
Julius Rudel: Guards! Guards! 34
Victor Alessandro: The "Time-Step" 38
Arturo Basile: "Chapaman" 39
Leonard Bernstein: "It's As If I Dreamed It" 41
Nadia Boulanger: Carissimi! It's a Forest Fire 42
Some Others: Hither and Yon 44

PHOTOGRAPH SECTION

The Pictures 48

THE SINGERS

Ritual Gestures and Nervous Habits 63
Sopranos 65
   Venora: The Soprano Who Peed Her Pants 67
   Butterfly: The Foot-in-Mouth Routine 68
Tenors 70
Baritones 73
Basses 75
   Fishing in Kodiak, Alaska 75
   The Tinkling Commendatore 75
   Very Sleepy Finale 76
   Favorite Fellows 77

OTHER CHARACTERS

Strange Students 81
The Agent 83
The Makeup Artist 85

About the Author 87
APPENDIX 93
Acknowledgments 133
Index 135

FOREWORD
Lunches with Herb
By David Mason

A friend is that rare creature with whom one never has to be on guard, one can always be oneself. I grew to love Herb Beattie not as an artist—though I love his voice and his wild stories about the artist's life—but as a man who sees the world in a big-hearted and accepting way, approaching it all first and foremost as a lover. We had known each other for years in Colorado Springs arts circles, but it was our shared devotion to poetry that first made us close friends. After we had both heard a triumphant reading by Richard Wilbur at Colorado College, Herb got ahold of me and suggested lunch. He wanted to talk about poetry. This would have been about 20 years ago, and we have been having lunch and sharing stories, poems, and songs ever since. Despite our age difference—Herb is physically older but younger in spirit—I consider him one of the great friends of my life.

 He never brags about his long and distinguished career as an operatic bass. Instead, he reveals it slowly, usually through humorous anecdotes. Born in 1926, Herb grew up in a real Chicago Irish family—lots of music and lots of stories. He served in the Navy before studying at Colorado College and the Mozarteum Salzburg. A true singer who can also act, he was often in demand with major opera companies all over the world, and he also had a long career as a music educator at American universities, particularly Hofstra, where one student he directed was none other than Madeline Kahn.

Though retired from his distinguished musical career when I got to know him, Herb was still working as a voice actor for advertisers, so lots of people heard his beautiful bass on radio and television without ever knowing they were listening to a genuine opera singer. Whenever we could find the time, he would pick me up at the college and drive me somewhere in the city for lunch, and there we regaled each other with stories about poets, musicians, and others we have known in our checkered lives. One of his lifelong friends, David Wagoner, is a poet I admire, and I loved hearing how as young men they connived a meeting with Dylan Thomas. Herb is that rare creature who actually reads poetry magazines—something most poets don't even do—and our conversations often ranged over the relative blandness of the current scene, our shared incredulity at how hard it is to find excellence in contemporary poetry. When I taught a class on the great poet W. H. Auden, Herb attended every day; my small group of students were treated to his readings of the poems, his stories about Auden's influence on modern literature. It's a fine thing for a professor to have a "student" in class more knowledgeable than himself. Teaching Auden's oratorio, *For the Time Being*, in a downtown coffee shop, I simply turned to Herb and asked him to explain what an oratorio was. He began with Bach, singing his quotations to rapt listeners, including the other customers in the cafe. The students adored him. The class ended with hugs all around.

Herb is a voracious reader. Our lunches are literary, as we share recommendations and opinions. So much of my reading has been for work—reviewing books or teaching them—so it is wonderful hearing about all the stuff he reads for the sheer pleasure of it and to mitigate his insomnia. We could talk James Joyce one day and Penelope Lively the next. Rare was the lunch in which I didn't hear something marvelously sung in German or Italian. When I started writing opera libretti, he was full of wonderful stories about how terrible the words are to most operas, what a pleasure it is to sing something well written. Our talks were head to head and heart to heart, full of shared delight. We've both had extra-literary experiences of travel and complicated family lives, so we've been able to support and encourage each other through all sorts of personal joys and tribulations.

Readers of this book are in for a treat—a small dose of what it's like to have lunch with Herb Beattie, to hear his stories and enjoy the freshness and breadth of a remarkable life. I've heard virtually all of these stories out loud, and reading them now in print I can promise you that he has caught the rhythms, humor, and intelligence of his oral storytelling perfectly. If you love music, you'll be amazed by the names—in a long career, Herb worked with many of the most significant classical musicians of the twentieth century. You'll feel the magic of getting a job from Leonard Bernstein, the tragicomedy of Pablo Casals intoning his philosophy of life even as he struggles on oxygen. The itinerant life of a working opera singer turns out to be full of characters and adventures, from playing off-stage ping pong with Danny Kaye to observing a conductor distractedly standing in the nude before a concert, and later having to inform the now-clothed gentleman that his fly is still undone. The sublimity of opera collides with the comedy of the "ordinary" human beings who make it happen.

Not many people can begin an anecdote like this: "Beverly Sills was sitting next to me on a flight from New York to Pittsburgh." Herb follows it with a marvelous story of singers entertaining each other before and during their performances. "I did an imitation of Zero Mostel's impression of a baby trying to find its thumb, which Bev really enjoyed." Sills responds with a joke about J. P. Morgan's bulbous nose. The joke comes to mind later, during their performance, when Sills points to their conductor's enormous nose, causing Herb to break into tears of hilarity midscene. (A reviewer took the tears for evidence of commendable grief.) It's the tragicomedy of art, and Herb's natural inclination to see the comedy first, even at his own expense, is one of the charms of this book.

I take particular pleasure in the detail he uses to describe his colleagues. He observes the conductor Kurt Herbert Adler, who "with his cool Viennese manner, his subtle, smooth, German-accented pronunciations, his handsome, Aryan, clean-cut face, his immaculate, fashionable costume topped off with the pipe clenched firmly in his teeth, gave one the feeling that he was not only in command of the *San Francisco Opera*, but that he was also a high-ranking officer in Rommel's North African Tank division." Virtually every personality in this book receives such close observation with the light touch of a true raconteur.

I encourage you to read these tales aloud in the plummiest voice you can muster, imitating all the accents and relishing the intelligent phrasings, the absurdity, the pratfalls, and fits of laughter. Then you will have some small idea of the many pleasures to be had during lunch with Herb Beattie.

The Life

THE LIFE

The phone rings and you can guess who is on the other end: none other than your New York best phone partner and agent, Ludwig Lustig. "Hello, Beattie—What about going to Ohio? They will love your Don Pasquale in Ohio."

That's the way it always begins. "Oh, sure," you say. Then the money is discussed, and you say, "Okay." It's that simple. And then you forget what it takes out of you. So begins the next odyssey of a traveling opera singer.

The Packing: Ye Gods!

The biggest problem of packing was to choose the right shoes for the roles I would be doing. I've often heard about the problem of shoes in opera. A famous soprano was asked by an interviewer why she was so vocally successful in long roles. Her answer was, "I had to have the right shoes or I couldn't sing the part." As a director I had the experience of a tenor in *Turandot* telling me he could not sing the high C unless he wore his own shoes. You can be sure the high C won out over the period shoes the costumer had chosen.

And it's true. Shoes make a huge difference to an opera singer. In some cases, I was allowed to choose my own shoes for a performance, rather than have the costumer dictate them. The ideal shoes had to be both comfortable and flexible, because in the comic roles in which I was often cast it was important to be able to move quickly on stage. But sometimes you find yourself at the mercy of the costumer, who can't rest until he (or she) straps you into some podiatric torture chambers for the sake of authenticity. The worst role for this is the Bonze in Puccini's *Madame Butterfly*. The offenders here are a sort of very unstable sandals with wooden strips vertically attached to the soles and heels (impossible to move quickly on, but supposedly traditional for priests of this period). They are made all the worse by your singing lines, which are short outbursts of "*maledizione!*" screamed out as you rush on stage. (Fortunately, the role is short, and you can rely on not taking a bow at intermission or being mentioned in a review.)

Aside from shoes, it is important to pack loose, comfortable clothes for rehearsals, which can seem interminable. The other essential is formal attire, because you are sure to be asked to attend wealthy donors' parties, where it is apparently important to make the impression that opera singers are all well off, which somehow stimulates giving rather than suggests that it is unnecessary!

The Traveling: Prepare to Die!

So now you have to get yourself to the gig. Travel arrangements are typically left up to you. I found that the best solution was usually to fly to the venue, even if it was within driving distance. Driving was frequently exhausting, resulting in a loss of energy that you would need for the rehearsal process and the performance. On the other hand, driving is the only option that allows you to practice your part on the way without upsetting your fellow travelers—well most of the time anyway. I remember several summers being engaged to sing in the opera in Central City, Colorado, and driving the 1,500 miles to there from our home in Long Island, New York, with my entire family of wife and five children in the family station wagon. Did I say exhausting? Yes! These trips have since become the stuff of family legend to my children. Lynn, my oldest daughter, remembers as a 13-year-old being embarrassed by her dear old dad practicing his scales as we sat at a red light in some little hamlet in Nebraska when a beautiful red convertible containing some "cool" and handsome teenaged boys pulled up next to us. As my voice rang out for several blocks, Lynn kept crouching closer and closer to the floor, mortified lest she be seen in my company! Lynn at the time had no use for opera, being a rock-and-roller all the way. "Got you, Lynn!" I said as the convertible sped off.

Flying, too, has its drawbacks, of course. The substantial odds that you could pick up a cold or worse from the stale, recirculating air in the cabin was an ever-present worry. The practice of wearing surgical masks, which some singers do these days, was not in vogue at the time and their efficacy is still questionable. You just took your chances and hoped that the tell-tale scratchy throat would hold off until the show was over.

Of course, any mode of travel takes its toll on your energy reserves. I generally dealt with jet-lag on overseas engagements well, probably due to natural good health and stamina, but for those who could afford it, arriving a few days early in order to become accustomed to the new time was not a bad idea. On the other hand, since many rehearsals were held in the evening, jet lag could be a short-lived advantage, as it would seem as though you were rehearsing in the morning by your own un-reset biological clock. Eventually, however, the time change would catch up with you and you just had to deal with it: "Do Not Disturb" signs on your hotel room door were your best friend as you struggled to catch up on sleep.

Arriving at the destination for the gig, I was typically met at the airport by an employee or volunteer of the organization that hired me. They would then take me to the designated lodging for us itinerant, wandering voices. Therein is another tale.

The Lodging: Are Those Bed Bugs?

Okay. So your lodging during the run of the show is usually assigned for you by the hiring organization. Sometimes the cost is on them, but often, in the smaller venues, it is up to you to pay for. Hotels were the typical choice, but occasionally the organization would have special homes for visiting artists, as they did in Tel Aviv. In Kentucky the organization actually provided a room not only for me, but for my children as well. This was also routinely the case in Central City, Colorado. My children loved the housing there as it was always some old Victorian, turn-of-the-century home with lots of doors and hiding places that was so different from our home in Long Island. The best part for the kids was that they could walk to the center of Central City where all the shops were without needing a ride. Being able to have your family on hand was a touching amenity that I greatly appreciated, as some engagements lasted weeks at a time.

My children also loved the Central City Opera because they were allowed to watch the rehearsals from backstage. One year, in *La Bohème*, four of them were even given parts in some of the crowd scenes. Mixing family life with your profession can have its hazards, though. I remember complaining privately about a fellow cast member being a "lush," only to hear my opinion broadcast the next day over the hall's PA system during rehearsal. It seems that the costume shop used the loudspeakers to call cast members back for costume fittings and generally kept the mic open. Thus, my daughter Lynn was visiting the costume shop and chatting with the costumer when she innocently repeated what I had said about the hapless cast member. She didn't even know what the word meant, but of course, I was mortified as all of us rehearsing on stage heard it!

But back to housing: The quality of the places we itinerant singers had to stay was all over the map, from sublimely shabby to five-star quality. Very occasionally, if the run of the rehearsals and show was long enough and the assigned lodging extremely subpar, I would endeavor to find an alternative on my own. This would sometimes lead to pleasant interactions with the natives, or to aggravating instances of mutual misunderstanding—something you wanted to avoid as the stress of the rehearsal process was already enervating to the point of making you crave solitude.

I remember when we were singing the opera *Susannah* by Carlisle Floyd with the New York City Opera at the Brussels World's Fair in 1958. Norman Treigle was playing the leading bass role of Blitch, the evangelical pastor, and I was one of the four, old, threadbare elders. Treigle and I had been given a room in the new quarters set up for the cast on the grounds of the fair. However, we decided to rent a local apartment when we realized that the rooms that had been given to us were hardly suitable. The toilet seat fell off the toilet, the walls were built of cardboard, and the light chain on the bedroom lamp fell out every time you pulled it. I remember the famous English actor George Coulouris, who was with the cast doing another show, stopping in and laughing with us about the state of these rooms. Treigle and I went out and found a nice apartment in the home of a local family within walking distance of the fair grounds.

On another occasion I was put up on the sixteenth floor of a nice hotel in San Francisco. The spectacular view had the unintended consequence of making me afraid of heights, which rendered my following gig in Vancouver quite dreadful. I was playing Dr. Dulcamara in Donizetti's *L'elisir d'amore* and I was to make my entrance descending from three stories up in a hot air balloon!

Sometimes the lodgings were adequate, but their location was a problem. On another occasion in San Francisco, we out-of-towners were put up in a hotel in a decidedly run-down and downright dangerous part of the city. Perhaps foolishly, I dealt with this issue after rehearsals and performances by sprinting from the performance hall to the hotel. I guess I hoped that my velocity would make would-be muggers look for easier targets, or think that I myself was up to no good and to be avoided. In any case, I lived to tell the tale, and the exercise was surely salutary.

The Food: Did the Laundry Shrink My Pants?

Having to eat out every meal for weeks during the rehearsals and run of a show is tiring, not to mention expensive and often unhealthy. Yet this was the typical arrangement on the road: Meals were up to you. Exceptions to this dismal routine did occur. In Tel Aviv a special cook was assigned to the visiting artists. This fellow happened to be a concentration camp survivor whose cooking was top notch. The best experience with food that I had, however, was in Rome where I was engaged to sing in the baroque opera *Sant'Alessio* by Stefano Landi for a long run of several weeks. The owners of a small *trattoria* where I often dined got wind that I was singing in the opera. From that day on they insisted on ushering me into the kitchen and preparing wonderful, exceptional meals just for me.

The worst food: Well, that had to be in Ohio. 'Nuff said.

The Payoff: Why Am I Here?

The answer always is: There is no other place I *could* be. From my earliest boyhood, singing and performing simply *were* me. I am mindful every day of my life of my good fortune in having both the talent and good training to make a career of it. The biggest screw-ups, the most irritating inconveniences, the deepest bone-weary exhaustion—it was all as nothing compared to the exhilaration of stepping out on stage into the magic of another world, bounded by a black region of space, where dimly seen—or more often felt—was the waiting audience. The wild pounding of my heart would suddenly sync with the music and I would *be* my part, forgetting all else, I was another person in another realm. Not always, but often enough, my fellow actors would be feeling it too, in the same frequency, and I and they would mesh exactly with the timing—not only of the music, but the dramatic action as well. And then, as if from another dimension, but as intimate as my own breath—which, in fact, it was—I would hear my own voice locking into a chord with such exquisite perfection that I knew that all the years of practice had culminated in this one moment, and the next and the next, as the flow of the music carried me forward like a wind of very heaven. And, when at last the show was over, I would land again, mortal and sweaty, on a stage I only dimly recognized, as exhausted I would drink up the roaring applause of the audience, loving them, loving all of life. There is simply nothing like it in the world.

And let us not forget all the little synchronicities that happen in every life, but which in the life of a performer can read like fairy tales—as, for example, the time that I, as the understudy's understudy to the role of Osmin in Mozart's *Abduction from the Seraglio*, was suddenly called to do the part. I had one hour to learn my role in English, but when the time came, I reverted to the original German to sing the famous aria, the language in which I had first learned it. In spite of that, I garnered a brilliant review from Harold Schonberg, the powerful music critic from the *New York Times*. To this day, the part of Osmin in this great Mozart opera is my favorite role to play. (My least favorite? The Bonz in *Madame Butterfly*, on account of those infernal shoes!)

Yes, those were the high highlights of the life of an opera singer, I suppose. But it also was often simply just a lot of good fun. And the cause of this has to be the shear plethora of characters who choose to make this their life's work—the sometimes unbelievable denizens that inhabit the weird, wonderful, whacky world of the operatic stage. Let's meet some of them.

The Conductors

THE CONDUCTORS

Josef Krips: "Ze Fly?"

I was behind the file cabinets on the other side of the room trying to be as unobserved as possible, struggling to get into my tuxedo. At the same time, I couldn't avoid peeking over the cabinets to see what the great conductor Joseph Krips was doing. Was he dressed already? Was he waiting for me? One could feel the magnetic presence of the great maestro no matter how far away he stood from you. On the podium before the orchestra and audience, he commanded your attention with his great musicianship, his huge person and personality. He dominated the area wherever he went, and now in this office of the music department at the University of Buffalo, his being there put everything else in miniature.

To get back to my peeking over the cabinets: My eyes were suddenly open to an amazing sight. There was Krips standing on the other side of the room, in full view of the open office windows, gazing quietly into space. He was wearing nothing except his black socks and black shoes—otherwise completely *nude*. Oh, yes, I forgot, he also had on his large Dr. Cyclops glasses perched on his sharp, turtle-beaked nose where he always wore them. His mouth, with its thin, straight line, hardly softened his moonlike face. His small, penetrating, watery eyes behind those glassy circles were magnified into large, blue, scary pools. (I remember the first violist, Fred Ressel, whispering into my ear during a 9:30 a.m. rehearsal of Handel's *Messiah* with Krips in Buffalo's Kleinhans Concert Hall, "How would you like two soft-boiled eyes for breakfast?")

Krips looked like the vision of a great baby whale with the shiny bald head of a man and two spindly, hairless legs supporting the largest belly you might hardly imagine. Yes, it was a vision beyond belief! And, below that stomach, there hung a large entangled mass of testicles that seemed to border on the intricacies of a curled-up, sleeping octopus. If you have ever been in the Rodin museum in Paris and seen the great sculptor's colossal nude of the writer Balzac, you might have some idea of what I was staring at.

I pulled on my tux and shirt and was adjusting my tie when I took another peek at the maestro. He was nearly dressed. But then, as he was pulling down his dress shirt, I noticed that *he was not wearing any underwear*. I was somewhat surprised, but thought that he was probably short on clean clothes, traveling between concert dates as much as he did. Or perhaps he simply enjoyed conducting without the confines of undershirt and briefs beneath his formal wear.

As I greeted him in mid-office space, I was suddenly shocked to see he had forgotten to zip up his trousers. I fumbled for a moment for words and took him by the sleeve. He said, "Vat, Beattie? Vat?" I blurted out, "The *fly*, ... the *fly!*" Krips looked at me quizzically and, looking up and around in the air, said, "Ze *fly*? ... Ze *fly*? ... *Vat* fly?" I said, "Oh, not *that* fly." And, pointing at his pants, "*That* fly!" Krips looked down, and seeing the wide open exposure, zipped up his zipper and said with a great sigh of relief, "Sanks Gott you tolt me!"

We walked slowly towards the stage and then he paused, turned to me, and said, "You know, Beattie, ven I vass conducting *Der Rosenkavalier* at ze Vienna Stadtsoper vun evenink, I noticed zer vass more laughing coming from ze singers und ze orchestra zan from ze audience. Looking down at ze principal cellist, I noticed as he vass bowing ze cello he vass also pointing mit ze bow at my pants. Ja, Beattie, ze *fly*! Ze *fly*!" And we went ahead and performed our music.

Peter Herman Adler: "You've Got to Be Kidding!"

Norman Treigle and I were sitting on the beds in our rented rooms trying to recover from a late evening at the Brussels World's Fair cafes. We were in Brussels to sing in the opera *Susannah* by Carlisle Floyd. However, between us lay the open score of the Richard Strauss opera *The Silent Woman*, which had just been sent to me. This was to be my assignment after we returned to New York. Treigle was looking at me with his customary jaundiced eye, saying, "They've got to be kidding!"

The score was almost the size of the New York City phone directory. The highest note for the bass voice was F above middle C, but the lowest note was a low C-sharp. Opera singers looking at a new opera they have been invited to sing usually—smartly—look at the range in the score to see if it fits their voice. Here, in the Strauss opera was an unbelievable range of over two octaves, and the staging directions called for the singer to sing the low C-sharp *off stage*. No wonder we started laughing. Besides, the opera was scheduled to open the fall season at the New York City Opera in September, and I was looking at this baby in June! In other words, six to eight weeks to learn a long, difficult opera.

Looking now at the 4-pound score, I realized that by giving into my agent's imprecations, I had stepped into a very large pile of commitment just over my head. No wonder Treigle said, "They've got to be kidding!"

After *Susannah* closed in Brussels, I flew off to Toronto to sing a small role in the *Song of Norway* for the tent theater on the Toronto fairgrounds and quickly forgot all about the *Silent Woman*. The *Song of Norway* was a two-week gig, and the only thing memorable about it was that during a performance I played ping pong with the actor Danny Kaye in the scene dock. He was doing his show at another venue at the fair and, growing tired of watching our show, asked me to play ping pong.

Two weeks later, at home in Buffalo, New York, I received a phone call from my agent, Ludwig Lustig, reminding me that I had agreed to sing the role of Sir Morosus Blunt in the upcoming New York City Opera production of *The Silent Woman*. We were well into July by that time and the premiere was to be the opening of the season in September. I quickly and loudly said into the phone, repeating Treigle's words, "They've got to be kidding!"

I had started to wonder what kind of brain I had to even consider this role. Any major role in an opera of Richard Strauss has got to take at least six months to learn. By this point, I had around six weeks. After a few weeks passed, I had developed muscle spasms in both arms from carrying the score around while studying it on the New York subways. I was beginning to get brain fever from looking at all the notes, and my voice was starting to mutter to me, "You've got to be kidding!"

Well, what does this have to do with Peter Herman Adler? It was Adler's idea. He was a puzzling "fountain of ideas," one of which was to open the fall season at the New York City Opera with this *Silent Woman* opera. Adler was a very influential conductor at the time, being director of the new NBC Opera Orchestra and a guest conductor at the New York City Opera with some real success in earlier productions. The *Silent Woman* would be an American premiere, and it was the kind of opera—being unknown to the opera-going public in New York City—that should draw a lot of attention in the press. Furthermore, its staging requirements were modest: a comic opera with singing actors, no chorus, a single setting, and a small orchestra befitting the eighteenth-century period in which it was set. It was a perfect fit for the repertoire for which the NYCO was known—something the Met wouldn't touch—and just right for the limited budget of Rudel's company. The libretto was written by Hugo von Hofmannsthal after a play by Ben Jonson. What could go wrong?

I found it was often strange working with Peter Herman Adler. He seemed too filled with ideas that he often had difficulty explaining to us poor singers. Although I had had sessions with the eccentric, but lovable, coach Kurt Saffir, I signed up for a special coaching session with Maestro Adler. When the time came, he rushed me off to his studio at the NBC Opera headquarters on 56th Street near Patelson's Music House, tore up the stairs, pushed me into his studio, put on a recording of Ezio Pinza singing old Italian art songs and, turning to me, clenched his teeth together, opened his mouth wide, and grimacing at me close to my face said, "Kreesch!!!" It was an expression I had never heard before. It was accompanied by a hand gesture near his mouth with a quick closing of his fist. He repeated it and then started the recording. As Pinza began singing, Adler quickly turned, and in a flash was gone. I sat there listing to the marvelous Pinza singing the Italian art song "*Gia sole dal gange*" of Scarlatti and the rest of the songs for about an hour and then, when no one came in to inform me of the maestro's wishes or the continuation of the session, I figured we were done and I wandered off, lonely and confused, onto 56th Street.

Well, it turns out that *The Silent Woman* was not the hit that Adler and the NYCO had expected—it was more of a curiosity in the Strauss genre. We sang three performances, and the production was retired, never to return to the NYCO stage.

Amazingly, the flight of this huge bird went off well enough, although I stumbled on my first entrance and skinned my shin so badly that it filled my shoe with blood. My adrenaline was so high that I didn't notice it until intermission. Margaret Webster, our fabulous director, was thoughtful and kind throughout the rehearsals. After the dress rehearsal, I sat on the stage completely downtrodden and nearly in tears, worrying about my ability to sing this opera. She came out on the set, put her arm around me, and said "Herbert, I know you are going to be wonderful. Don't worry about a thing." And I smiled and kept thinking, "You've got to be kidding!"

William Steinberg: Te Deum or Tedium

It seems hardly possible that a single phrase or a word remembered in a serious situation could set one off into an uncontrollable state of laughter. But it can! But let me relate the whole story.

Beverly Sills was sitting next to me on a flight from New York to Pittsburg. We were booked by our agent, Ludwig Lustig, to sing the solos in Anton Bruckner's great sacred chorale *The Te Deum* with the Pittsburg Symphony, William Steinberg conducting. I had learned my part in about half an hour, as it was short and consisted mainly of a number of "amens."

The soprano and tenor solos are extensive and require first-class artists, hence Beverly and a tenor named William Dembaugh. Anyway, Sills and I were chatting and laughing, telling jokes and enjoying one another. I did an imitation of Zero Mostel's impression of a baby trying to find its thumb, which Bev really enjoyed. In response, she began telling me a joke about J. P. Morgan at a private dinner with the socially prominent Lowell family at their home in Boston. The Lowells made extravagant warnings to their children to be extra careful with regards to J. P. Morgan's unusually large nose—not to look at it or say anything about it, and to be very subdued throughout dinner. If they disobeyed, the children understood they would be shut in a closet for some time or sent away to a distant unsympathetic relative. The story, probably apocryphal, goes on to relate how everything went fine until the first course at dinner when the youngest child sitting next to J. P. said to him, "Please pass the nose." I laughed and forgot the joke—until later when it reappeared in my memory at the very wrong moment.

I had hardly entered into preparations for the *Te Deum*, so during my ample free time I wandered over to Forbes Field, which was very close by my hotel, and watched the Pirates play several games. During the few rehearsals I attended, it was evident that William Steinberg was still mourning the death of his lovely wife, Lotte, who had died several months before. The performances were to be solemn affairs fitting the mood of the conductor.

At last, there I was in performance, gazing at my score, waiting for my few solos, when I looked over at Sills. She caught my eye and then looked at the conductor, who was waving his baton at the orchestra. I saw nothing amiss and looked back at Beverly. She looked at me and again at Steinberg and again at me with what I detected as a kind of arching of her eyebrows. Suddenly my solo came up and I jumped to my feet to sing. The text I was about to sing shot off the page and into my mind with amazing significance. I sang the words "*super nose.*" It means "upon us" in Latin, but I was fixated on what it *sounded like* in English. Naturally Beverly's joke came into my mind instantly, and I found myself looking at Steinberg's enormous honker. As the laughter welled up inside me, for a second all I could do was grit my teeth and hold on for dear life. My eyes began to water and tears roll down my cheeks. I sat down after an "amen" and realized I had made it through the crisis with hardly any notice. I did not dare to look at Beverly throughout the final movements of the work. I wondered after the concert that no one said anything to me. The next morning the review in the paper read in part: "The bass was so moved that he was in tears."

Eugene Ormandy: Thus Saith the . . . Conductor

I have seldom been caught in a situation where delicate politicking is necessary. But here was a seemingly easy situation that turned out to be a bit nerve wracking when it came to protocol—or, let's just say, trying to do the right thing.

It was 9 a.m. and Eugene Ormandy walked into the backstage area of the Academy of Music in Philadelphia with the orchestra's accompanist. I followed as we quickly went into the maestro's private dressing and rehearsal suite.

Ormandy was always on time and projected in his three-piece suit the image of a successful businessman on his way to the stock market. Of course, a conductor must have a certain degree of ego to do the job, but Ormandy's was colossal. I recall on a different occasion when I was singing *The Childhood of Christ* by Berlioz under Ormandy's direction, my son Mark and daughter Dawn were in attendance. Dawn, being only a small child at that time, fell asleep during the first half, and Mark brought her backstage during intermission. Seeing the sleepy child, Ormandy said to Mark: "Let her sleep on my chaise in my dressing room. That will give her a story to tell when she grows up—that she slept in Ormandy's room."

But back to the story at hand: The scene is Ormandy's private rehearsal room at the Academy of Music in Philadelphia at 9 a.m. We were about to run through some of the passages for bass in Handel's *Messiah* so that we could agree before the morning rehearsal as to how we would perform this music.

As we set up for the run-through, I was slightly alarmed by the fact that there was a distinct smell of alcohol coming from the gentleman sitting at the piano. The close quarters of the room made it clear as to where this odor was coming from, and I looked to see if the pianist was looking hung over. It was obvious that he had had a bad night and, from the expression on his face and his very bleary red eyes, it was clear that he was wishing to be anywhere else in the world than looking at the opening recitative for the bass voice in the too-often-performed *Messiah* on a Saturday morning at 9 a.m. with Eugene Ormandy hovering over him.

I was hoping nothing would be said and that the session would begin and end as quickly as possible. The *Messiah* is a great work, of course, but it is performed way too often. In Britain it is sung hundreds of times at Christmas and Easter, and apparently that tradition continues to keep lots of musicians well-funded for the holidays. I remember the often repeated story about the English violinist who said, "I dreamt I was playing *Messiah* and I woke up, and I *was!*"

When I was an undergraduate in Colorado Springs, I was the bass soloist at a church that provided the backup music to the Easter Sunday 6 a.m. service at the Garden of the Gods that was broadcast nationally over the CBS network. If there was rain or snow and the service was cancelled at the park, we, the choir at Grace Episcopal Church, provided a program of Easter music as a filler. I was slated to sing the bass solo "The Trumpet Shall Sound" from *Messiah*. The piece is within comfortable range if you happened to be a baritone, but for the bass, it offers lots of high E's, and that means you had better be well warmed up, rested, and unusually confident when you wail into it. I was none of these and fortunately the regular service went as scheduled. But for the rest of my singing career, whenever the *Messiah* raised its sacred head, I shuddered thinking of that aria. As it turned out, I shuddered frequently as everyone always wanted *Messiah* at Christmas.

But to get on with it: There we were, scores at the ready. I was looking at the petite figure of the great conductor Eugene Ormandy, waiting for his downbeat, breathing the leftover ingestions of scotch whisky from the accompanist at 9 a.m. Saturday morning at the Academy of Music in Philadelphia. At the conductor's gesture, the accompanist played the first chords of the introduction to the recitative "Thus Saith the Lord." Everything would have been fine if he had played the chords in the key of D minor as written by George Frideric Handel, but as it happened, he played those harmonies in D major. I looked at Ormandy, expecting him to correct the pianist, *but he did not*! I hesitated. I could see Ormandy looking at me with the expectation of hearing my voice. In the fraction of a second before the overtones of the mistaken D major chord faded away, my mind was whirring: *What shall I sing? Major or minor? Or should I tattle to Ormandy on my fellow musician suffering at the keyboard?* "Hey! He played the wrong chords!" *But what if Ormandy himself doesn't know the difference between major and minor in this piece? Then it would be insulting to the great maestro to point it out. But what if he's just trying to see if I know the difference? Either way it could be so embarrassing that I'll never be engaged again by him for any performances.* Well, I was too frightened to do anything, so—not saying a word—I sang "Thus Saith the Lord" in the wrong key of D major and just went ahead as if nothing had happened.

So much for the *Messiah*. The performances went well, and we all (the orchestra and I) performed the recitative and aria just as Handel had written it—in D minor. The lesson here is: Burying one's head in the sand is sometimes a good idea under certain circumstances.

Pablo Casals: Oxygen

My agent called me and asked me to send a tape to Pablo Casals so that he could hear my voice. Fine! Great! A chance to sing with the great Casals! I was also to make the songs on the tape something contemporary. Okay. So I sent some Ives and Copland songs and waited. Apparently these selections didn't show off my voice well enough for the maestro, so he told my agent I should sing some Brahms or Schubert. The next call from my agent said the tape was fine and I was engaged to sing Casals's oratorio *El Pessebre* at Florida State University a few months later.

My first rehearsal with Casals was at 10 a.m. at our hotel in Tallahassee near the university. I had listened to him practicing his cello earlier that morning and this added to my nerves. (I thought, "*How will I sound in person? He's only heard me on tape.*") By the time 10 a.m. rolled around and I was knocking on the maestro's hotel door, I was in a state of the jitters. The door opened and greeting me was a beautiful young lady, dressed in white. I thought for a moment that I was at the wrong door and that the figure before me was an angel from on high. She quickly assured me she was real by inviting me in. This she did in the most mature way and told me that the maestro was waiting in the sitting room.

And there he was, sitting in the middle of a couch smoking one of his many meerschaum pipes. He waved me over to sit next to him and asked me to tell him about myself. He was very friendly and smiling, and as I sat down on the couch next to him my nerves began to settle down. I told him I was married and had four children. He nodded warmly at this news and, patting his chest, murmured something under his breath. Encouraged by this response, I thought I would win even more approval by telling him that the first thing I did in the morning was to go to the piano with my eldest son and read through some Bach preludes and fugues from the *Well-Tempered Clavier*. I thought I couldn't go wrong with this, as Casals's playing of Bach was legendary, and his recordings of Bach were considered definitive. Suddenly Casals said "Oh no! You must first go out into the garden and love the flowers, love the trees, love the sky, love the grass. Then go in and have breakfast. *Then* Baaaccch!"

Alexander Schneider, the very important music valet to Casals, was in San Salvador for several weeks rehearsing the orchestra for the performance of the oratorio in Florida. The orchestra was made up of musicians from all over Central America as well as El Salvador. They were instructed that any late arrivals to rehearsals—not to mention no-shows—would be facing at least a night in jail or worse. There was one important passage in the orchestral part of the work that involved a transition section from the woodwinds to the strings plus a change of tempo. Let me try to write it out for you:

Woodwinds (flutes, oboes, clarinets) in an ascending scale: beep, bee beep, beep, beep—pause. This was followed by a continuation upwards of that scale: beep, bee beep, beep, beep. A quarter rest held slightly, then a downward rush of the violins into a six-eight sort of quick tarantella in the low cellos and basses. Schuh, schuh, schuh, schuh, schuh, schuh, schuh, schuh schuh ... bump, buh bump, buh bump ...

Fairly simple you say? Not for the musicians in Central America. Schneider had to rehearse this section over and over, and it gave him something of a headache as to the hope of its exact execution in performance.

The stage in the brand new movie house on the evening of the performance was ample for the forces involved for *El Pessebre*: a full orchestra; 5 soloists and a choir of 200 young, smiling, Salvadorians in their white shirts and blouses, arranged on risers behind the orchestra, the dark-skinned faces smiling brightly with wide smiles and gleaming white teeth. At the rear of the stage-left entrance, placed as inconspicuously as possible, was a screen behind which sat several chairs and a large cylinder of oxygen with a connected mask. This small, secreted section was placed where it was so that it would be available in case Casals was in need of it. The evening was very warm and the temperature on the stage probably over 90. The first half of the concert was conducted by Schneider and the maestro was kept backstage.

After the intermission, Pablo Elvira, the baritone, and I at each arm escorted Casals to the podium. The maestro patted his chest and murmured, "love, love, love," as he smiled kindly to the orchestra and the chorus. Everyone looked happy and reassured by these words and gestures as the apparently kind and loving conductor, composer, and great cellist took his chair and raised his baton. He gave an upbeat, and the basses played a single note, a low E-natural. He gave a clear cue, and to everyone's amazement—certainly Casals's—the chorus, instead of beginning the consonant E major harmony of the chorale, found a series of unrelated pitches and began singing what was something like a late dissonant work that could only be a passage from Arnold Schönberg's opera *Moses and Aaron*. Suddenly Casals's temperament changed from the kindly, loving father of the downbeat to a ferocious angry mother bear. He rose to his feet and, pawing at the air, seemed to be flailing at the chorus, trying to whip the correct music out of their mouths instead of what he was hearing. When the short chorale finally reached its none-too-soon-for-all-concerned strangled cadence, Casals in one motion turned to me and, clutching his heart, struggled off the podium. Elvira and I grabbed him, escorting him back to the screened-in section on the platform as he breathlessly whispered to us, "Oxygen! Oxygen! Oxygen!" Behind the screen his wife Martita and a physician quickly set the maestro into a large, comfortable chair and—having put the oxygen mask on him—turned the valve on the oxygen tank.

There was a good deal of murmuring from the audience. The soloists, chorus, and orchestra sat still and waited to see what would happen next. Suddenly from the wings Alexander Schneider walked to the podium and took over conducting *El Pessebre*. Everything quieted down and went as planned, and the excerpt from *Moses and Aaron* was forgotten. Behind the screen there was silence as the sound of hissing air stopped—until the troubling section at the rehearsal mentioned above appeared in the score. Schneider mumbled worriedly under his breath, his eyes suddenly large and staring. His general demeanor was that of a tragic figure in a play, waiting for the worst possible news to befall his ears. The woodwinds fell to the occasion, lost all their composure, stumbled through the rising scale and shook the string section so badly that they slipped and stuttered through the six-eight measures that introduced the tarantella rhythm in the basses. From behind the screen we heard Casals cry out, "Oxygen! Oxygen! Oxygen!"

Dr. John Finley Williamson: The Disappearing Conductor

Choral conducting is in a class by itself. A symphony conductor has personnel of perhaps 60 to 100 players to command, a large number of whom not only disagree with the conductor, but actually wish him or her the very worst that they can think up—from departures to alien planets to long and painful illnesses ending in certain death. But, as I said, choral conducting is in a class all by itself. Most all the singers in choruses *love* their conductors and would practically sacrifice their lives for them.

Many choral conductors find that using only their hands to conduct gives the choral singer a better feeling for the vocal experience that the conductor wants to elicit than conducting with a baton. Using only hand gestures, a choral conductor can more easily mold the vocal flow, shaping the phrases and drawing forth the words that are being sung. The vocal conductor also provides breath support for the singers by breathing in sync with them, bringing all the conductor's empathy to the group. This is extremely important. Symphony conductors most often engage special choral conductors (the exception being Robert Shaw) to prepare the music when a choir is performing with the symphony. These conductors have developed brilliant choruses that are famous for their sound and musicianship. My particular subject for this short essay is the famous choral conductor Dr. John Finley Williamson.

Williamson created the Westminster Choir and the famous Westminster Choir College (formerly Westminster Choir School) in Princeton, New Jersey. He was, above all else, a dynamic personality who left his imprint upon thousands of teachers and graduates from the Choir College. With a great head of flowing white hair, handsome features, piercing blue eyes, athletic figure, and clear voice, he was a person of dramatic, commanding stature. He also possessed the charm of a fine diplomat and the iron fist of an administrator and teacher. In short, he was a fantastic force of power and strength. And he was a phenomenal choral conductor.

Williamson's ideas could be challenged on many levels, but when he introduced a new composer to the faculty one Thursday at chapel service, everyone took his words seriously. Williamson spoke of Roy Harris as a great American composer who was finally coming to Westminster as Composer in Residence. Roy then got up and sauntered over to the gospel side of the altar to give his answer to Williamson's flowery introduction. In his Oklahoma-accented, drawling way, he imparted the surprising information that "there's only one thing you can depend upon, and those are the seasons. They come around every year," and then sat down. Dr. Williamson, somewhat nonplussed with these sentiments, grew red-faced and fluttery as he quickly dismissed the students from the chapel.

I was a graduate student at the Westminster Choir School from 1948 to 1950, studying composition with Normand Lockwood. I was also in the prestigious Westminster touring choir that sang concerts all over the United States. We were in Tulsa, Oklahoma, singing a concert in a very large Baptist church. I remember that the apron of the platform had been extended with fake flooring, so that the limited depth of the stage would have the appearance of a regular stage platform. Dr. Williamson was warned backstage before his entrance to stay close to the choir's position upstage on the platform, because the front (downstage) portion of the newly enlarged platform was very unstable and to step on it could prove disastrous. Apparently in the preconcert preparations, the maestro forgot this advice.

The choir was on stage, on time, all 24 singers in concert dress, smiling at the packed audience and ready to launch into the Heinrich Schütz motet for double choir. Dr. Williamson came briskly out of the wings, smiling, his face filled with great purpose and confidence. He did not stop at the prearranged spot before the choir, but strode forward. And in a few steps, he disappeared before our eyes.

The audience gasped. The singers stood stunned and frozen for what seemed an unbelievable length of time. But before anyone could do anything, the hands of the conductor suddenly appeared at the edge of the stage and—pulling himself up in a quick athletic bounce—Dr. Williamson was again before us. He looked at the choir, his face white as a sheet, and gave the downbeat for the opening work. The choir responded without a hitch and our voices rang out in the Schütz motet. It was terribly interesting to me to watch Dr. Williamson's unbelievable showmanship in holding his whole body together, poised and as if nothing had happened, energetically continuing the performance. After about 10 minutes and well into another work, I saw that our conductor's face had turned back to its usual ruddy color. At the close of the piece, he turned and, smiling, acknowledged the warm applause greeting him. He was the most completely assured, controlled conductor I have ever seen.

Sarah Caldwell: What Will Happen Next?

If you were invited to sing for the Opera Company of Boston in the second half of the twentieth century, you knew you were in for something very unusual. You had to be prepared for a number of things that were often quite different from any other opera company out there on American stages. First and foremost, you were going to learn new pieces—or at least pieces that were rarely performed. You would be dealing with one of the most courageous and inventive minds in the world of opera. You would know you had been chosen by Sarah Caldwell because she saw something in you that was more than the usual opera singer. Sure, you had a good voice, but more than this, you were a good musician and you could act. You could follow her ideas and she would enjoy collaborating with you in working out the role with her concept. True, there were times when she would start one place and end up in a completely different one. But this was so refreshing after working with conductors and directors who were set in their ideas about how this or that scene should be staged or sung. Sarah was always up for a new and exciting way of doing opera. It is true that many directors in opera did not have the luxury of time, money, and cast choice to bring new things to the repertory, and—let's face it—opera audiences (God bless them!) are often very set in their ways about how the opera in question should be presented. This, of course, is due to the repetition of "bread and butter repertoire"—that is, *Bohème, Tosca, Madame Butterfly, Traviata, Carmen, Fledermaus, Aida, Rigoletto, Cavalleria rusticana, Pagliacci, Barber of Seville,* and *Faust*. Audiences love these operas because they have seen them more than any others and have learned what they are about and what the singers are singing. It's also fun to hear different singers in the same roles and compare their voices. The opera audience is first and foremost interested in the sounds the singers are making. Who cares about the art of the music?

But in Sarah Caldwell's career this made all the difference. She consistently put on operas that were distinctly new to the audience. Of course, this was Boston! And the audience for music in Boston was quite different. Highly educated, sophisticated, opinionated, and snobbish, they were delighted that Sarah was their girl on the podium.

I did *The Marriage of Figaro* with her (Dr. Bartolo) with an all-black cast as the servants and white honkeys like me as the people in charge (although she hired a Countess whom she had never met, and the wonderful singer who showed up was black!) and it was as exciting a performance of *Figaro* as you would ever see.

At another time we did a series of performances of the Berlioz *Les Troyens* and I got to see a scene in which my face, filmed, filled the entire backdrop as the ghost of Hector (I loved it). Then there was *I Capuleti e i Montecchi* with Beverly Sills and Tatiana Troyanos as Romeo and Juliet. Before the last scene at the tomb during the first performance, Sarah called Robert Trehy and me (playing Lorenzo and Capellio) into her dressing room and told us she wasn't sure we could get through the iron gate at the top of the tomb scene because it was probably latched on the inside and in order to get through it we would have to break it down. This information struck both Bob and me with an attack of panic that suddenly enlivened our roles as the two old fathers of the doomed lovers. It took some extra adrenaline and a lot of pushing and silent cursing to get that gate open, but we did it, and I think the audience was impressed with our seemingly "actors' studio" realism. The criticism that I got for my role as the elder Capulet was that "his voice was as grey and woolly as his beard." Nice reward for an on-stage necessary improv.

Ah, yes—the unexpected moments in opera!

Kurt Herbert Adler: Charming!

Der schöne Adler was a whole opera world unto himself. The most handsome of all *intendants*, soft spoken, exquisitely dressed, a soft Viennese accent, a pipe in his mouth—the air of an aristocrat and the heart of a prison warden. With one hand he built the San Francisco Opera into a world-renowned theater equal to the splendor of the great city it represented.

I was engaged as Don Alfonso in *Così fan tutte* in the spring season of the company. Maestro Adler let the marvelous stage director and music coach Bliss Hebert go about his plan for a different approach to this masterpiece, which was often directed in strange settings and even stranger costumes. We worked on an idea for three weeks that Bliss had conceived as a kind of chess game on a large chess board with the two pairs of lovers as knights and queens under the control of the sinister magician/chess master, Don Alfonso. I loved this idea because Alfonso is often staged as a philosophical, dispirited crank who looks despairingly on all episodes involving young love. He is rather reduced to a shade on the stage because he has little music to sing. The part can be strengthened by staging and singing. In Hebert's vision, Alfonso really becomes a pawn himself when the subjects begin to exert their passions and become more and more free of his cynical philosophy.

Our rehearsals went well and swiftly, and the singers, stage director, and assistant conductor were well pleased that the new concept was taking shape and developing into a strong and quite original concept for this masterpiece. But—alas—all was to change, quickly and drastically. *Der schöne Adler* had not appeared for any of our rehearsals: a busy, busy man trying to run a spring season with young, unknown artists and who knows what concepts of brainy directors? Then, at almost the final run-through stage rehearsal, without costumes or orchestra, Adler appeared. With his singular aristocratic tone he interrupted our rehearsal and, speaking to all of us, told us that the presentation was "*not charming!*" Of course, we were concentrating on a completely different approach to the opera that we thought would be appealing as a new concept of this work. After all, it can get a bit hackneyed after years of the same romantic charades. But we hurriedly (and I could say *frantically*) restaged and redid *Così fan tutte* as a *charming* opera.

Emerson Buckley: Buck

To move from Kurt Herbert Adler to Emerson Buckley is like crossing the equator at least five times. Adler, with his cool Viennese manner, his subtle, smooth, German-accented pronunciations, his handsome, Aryan, clean-cut face, his immaculate, fashionable costume topped off with the pipe clenched firmly in his teeth, gave one the feeling that he was not only in command of the San Francisco Opera, but that he was also a high-ranking officer in Rommel's North African Tank division.

Buckley, however, in Central City, Colorado, as music director of the opera company and its chief conductor, fit the western scene as a fish to water. He wore a ten-gallon hat, a bow tie, a checked shirt, Levi's held up with an enormous Indian belt buckle, and sported a continuously lit cigarette, the yellow stain of which had colored his full mustache and even fuller goatee. His language was—putting it lightly—*colorful*, expressing the many points of an opera score or a singer's singing with some of Henry Miller's bluer expressions in *Tropic of Capricorn*. He also had a habit of never calling you by your name. Instead, you might have to answer to any of a number of vulgar epithets, which would change from day to day as he ordered you about the stage like some sort of sadistic first mate on a sailing ship. He spoke quickly, running the words closely together through the cigarette smoke and whiskers, so that you were not always sure that what he had just said was what you thought he had said.

Buckley fit perfectly into the western mining town of Central

City, like an "Old Cowhand from the Rio Grande." But, *but*, he was a master at rehearsing and conducting opera. His conducting cues were absolutely clear, strong, and decisive. Throughout every rehearsal you went through with him, there was no doubt as to when your entrance was and at what dynamic. If you did not feel prepared for a performance with Emerson Buckley, there was decidedly something wrong with you. I never felt in doubt about when to come in musically when I sang opera with him. I'm sure there were times when he was exasperated with the singer or pit orchestra player, but I have never worked with a more consistently clear conductor of operas in my career. True, he may not have had the taste you would have appreciated in preparing and performing opera, but his repertoire was always at his complete control and he was wonderful to work with.

He knew singers inside and out. He knew when and how to work with them and his performances were always spotless musically. He did have differences with stage directors—but who didn't? Certain ideas were traditional in the staging of the popular repertoire and those stage directors who went off the deep end with their ideas were firmly rebuked and argued heatedly with at every turn. Operas in Central City always had the shortest preparation periods, and so it was expedient to move quickly and firmly in proven directions.

On one occasion I was entertaining a relative of mine who had never been in an opera house before, showing him the stage and auditorium at Central City. We were admiring the old beauties of the decor, the great works of opera, the aesthetics of the masterworks, when suddenly, without warning, two figures appeared on the stage together, walking briskly from one side to the other.

They were speaking in loud voices and discussing differences of opinion with some of the roughest language I hadn't heard since my days as a Naval apprentice seaman. My guest looked at me with some astonishment and was about to speak when the arguing duo appeared again, this time from stage right and, again speaking loudly with a whole new set of unfamiliar vulgarity, then disappeared stage left. "Yes," I said to my astonished guest, "that's also opera."

Josef Krips once told me that to stay in an opera house in Germany for more than three years was a miracle. There are so many problems with putting on opera that the medium itself destroys relationships among artists—if not immediately, then certainly within a short period of time.

Julius Rudel: Guards! Guards!

Julius Rudel, the absolute *intendant*/conductor/coach/artistic director was responsible for doing the most impossible, amazing feat in the history of American opera. He steered the New York City Opera for 25 years through all kinds of desperate raging seas and storms with unfailing faith, strength, and astounding success. No one in the history of American opera has ever done anything close to this singular achievement. He was patient (with singers like me) and adventuresome. He produced more new operas than any artistic director in the United States. He engaged young, new singers at the City Center and he brought in a line of directors from legitimate Broadway stage theater to give new life to an old tradition. He had the most remarkable memory. I remember during rehearsals, Julius would remember details of staging of a former production of a year or two back that the cast hardly remembered. He pointed it out and it was invariably correct and added always to the overall success of the production.

Rudel could overlook unlikely things that happened in performance, as conductors and stage directors often have to do in opera. I remember when we were doing the *Abduction from the Seraglio* at the Mozart Festival at Stanford University in California. The cast was pretty much the same singers as in New York except for the Pasha. In this case, the role was given to a movie actor with a marvelous reputation for scary roles—Albert Dekker, by name. His wonderful voice, commanding stature, and riveting presence was an immediate plus for the production. The Pasha in *Abduction* is a speaking role and a pivotal one. He must turn the tables on the plot by granting the abducted characters (Konstanze, Blonde, Pedrillo) their freedom, releasing them from his hold at the last minute as the act of a generous and intelligent ruler. Dekker was totally convincing, although he had an original concept of the lines he was to deliver—not that the translation of the original text was any good anyway. But whether Dekker did not ever really memorize these words or simply felt he was better at extemporizing the role I have never been sure. I think what he thought up was better than the original anyway.

In rehearsals for *Abduction from the Seraglio*, the cast was reminded again and again to avoid stepping on the bar that held the flats up that was situated at the entrance portal of the set. This set had been used in New York City for this production, but it was secured by the usual lines for the *indoor* stage—*not the outdoor* stage that we were using in Stanford. The upshot was that if you happened to step on this bar, the flats for this section of the set would lose their balance (achieved by propped-up sandbags) and come falling down.

Dekker, with all his marvelous costuming as the Pasha (including the tiny knives he had taped to his wrists, which he said was a detail he had researched), his stentorian, ad-libbed lines, and great bravura acting promptly made his entrance through the ill-fated portal on opening night, stepped on the aforementioned bar—and turned to see the flat toppling over towards him. Without a single hesitation, being the consummate stage and screen actor he was, Dekker rushed back to the panel, and throwing his hands up in the air stopped the set in mid-fall, declaiming loudly, "Guards! Guards!" I was standing in the wings with John White (managing director at the New York City Opera) and when we witnessed this series of events we could not contain ourselves from rolling with laughter on the floor. (I'm not sure what Rudel's reaction was, as he was conducting, but I assumed he wasn't quite as amused as we were, but he went right on with the show.)

A worse infraction involving unscripted laughter occurred during a performance of the American opera *Susannah* by Carlisle Floyd at the Brussels World's Fair in 1958, also conducted by Rudel. In this case I was completely unhinged by the tenor Michele Molese's whispered remark to me during the picnic scene. Molese, Chet Ludgin, and I (the Elders) were doing our best to shun Susannah when she appeared with a bowl of peas at the gathering. We were all immobile in stances with frozen facial frowns. The next line was sung by the late, wonderful contralto Ruth Kobart. Ruth made no mistake when she sang the line, "I wouldn't tech them peas uh her'n." The power of her projection was amazing. The saliva that flew from her mouth as she projected the consonants "t" and "p" ran out over the stage and orchestra pit into the first rows of the audience. It was memorable. It was beyond comprehension, it was a moment to be remembered forever by each member of the cast.

An aside here: The problem of oral projectiles is actually a "thing" with some singers, and I myself was not immune. The problem frequently stems from directors with some cockeyed idea that your mouth should be doing something more than just singing.

A friend of mine who was a young chorus singer at the time remembers me in the role of Leporello in *Don Giovanni* in Colorado Springs, during which I was required to sing and eat an enormous leg of turkey at the same time. Some 40 years later he remembers bits of macerated turkey flying everywhere, and the trauma of being in their path still has not left him. Once, when I was playing Mustafa in *An Italian Girl in Algiers* by Rossini, the director had me chew on a date and then dramatically spit out the pit when I commenced singing. And then there was the time in *Street Scene* by Kurt Weill: I was playing the part of Frank Maurrant, and the director wanted me to be smoking a cigarette from which I would take a huge drag and exhale a dramatic plume of smoke right before I began to sing. This was tricky, and one night I accidentally lit the wrong end of the cigarette. It did not go well.

Food props in opera are common: Many operas include scenes at dinner tables. The "food" is usually artificial. In one production of *An Italian Girl in Algiers* we had a large bowl of "spaghetti" artfully fashioned from a mass of tangled string with painted sauce. On closing night a strange compulsion seized me and I grabbed the bowl of this stuff and emptied it over the head of the conductor, a dear friend. After a stunned moment, the audience went wild. Too bad it was the last performance. That stunt might have made its way into the permanent stage directions.

But back to *Susannah* and Ruth Kobart: At the final performance I was a bit unsteady, having spent several previous late nights with Norman Treigle enjoying the caprices and flowing wines of the "Belgiek Joyeus" on the main street of the fair grounds. Just before Ruth's famous line, Molese, who was facing upstage and to my left, as I faced directly into the audience and the conductor, Julius Rudel, whispered to me, "*Here it comes.*" My composure went out the window. I stopped being the shunning Elder I was supposed to convey to the audience and simply broke down into an insane fit of laughter. Regaining my self-control, I quickly resumed my role for the rest of the opera. After the final curtain, I rushed out the backstage door, cursing the tenor Molese under my breath, and hoping to miss running into Rudel. He never said anything to me about this episode and to this day I have never brought the matter up to anyone except my closest friends.

Victor Alessandro: The "Time Step"

The conductor Victor Alessandro of the San Antonio Opera invited Beverly Sills to come to his stage and do her wonderful performance of Rosina in *The Barber of Seville*. Bev (known as "Bubbles" to her friends) brought some of her buddies along to round out a cast of singers who she knew could and would get laughs in the well-known opera. I was one of those guys doing my Don Bartolo, and Arnold Voketaitis was feeding me the right stuff singing Don Basilio.

At one of the first piano rehearsals, Bubbles and I got into a conversation about our childhood learning experiences concerning the stage. We agreed that taking tap dancing lessons at age seven was one of those learning experiences that helped somewhat later in doing comic opera. I asked her if she knew the "time step" and she said, "Of course!" The step is basic in the repertoire of any kid who puts on a pair of patent leather tap shoes and velvet pants.

Well, Bev and I were hoofing it up with our "time step" when Maestro Alessandro walked in. He watched for a moment and then, scratching his head, said to us, "*Questa quella?*" We told him about the "time step" and he, looking puzzled and smiling, said "Where does dis tima steppuh happen in *Il barbiere di Siviglia?*" He was a perfect example of a purely opera-trained Italian conductor and we loved him. We decided not to put the "time step" into any scene in *The Barber of Seville* and I think the audience and Victor thought those performances were terrific anyway.

Arturo Basile: "Chapaman"

At the close of the New York City Opera's stay at City Center Theater on 55th Street in the late 1950s, there were many reasons why the directors engaged opera conductors from Europe. Well versed in the standard repertoire and seemingly at ease working with American singers (although sometimes not, as you will see) and early in their careers (which made them not too highly paid for NYCO's slim budget), they offered very special reasons for their engagement at the aspiring young company. One of the most successful of these was the marvelous and often funny Arturo Basile. (I saw him floating paper airplanes from his conductor's podium during a piano dress of Verdi's *Macbeth*). Today Basile's recordings are much sought after.

We had finished rehearsing *Macbeth* and it was opening night. The role of Macbeth was sung by the young American bass-baritone William Chapman. The director was the incredible Shakespearian scholar Margaret Webster. She had made the chorus wear large numbered place cards around their necks for rehearsals. An almost all-American cast (except for Giuseppe Gismondo, who played Macduff and had trouble hearing the orchestra because the helmet the costume department gave him had metal flaps over his ears) sang in Italian. This was to be a special evening for the City Opera. And it was in many ways.

I was singing the small role of Sicario, a cutthroat of Macbeth's. I, in long cloak, large hat, and ugly makeup, with obvious blood on my hands, was stage right out on the right wings of the stage, whispering *"egli mori"* to Macbeth to let him know that Banquo was indeed dead. However, Chapman never got a cue from Basile, so we stood there for a one minute silently pantomiming a secret conversation while the entire ensemble was at the banquet table singing and reveling in food and wine. After a moment I left, and Macbeth went back to his festivities. My important information to Macbeth of Banquo's death went unexpressed and hence made the appearance a bit later of Banquo's ghost at the table somewhat meaningless. Laughingly I asked the coach in the wings, "Should I take a curtain call?"

But Basile was furious at Bill Chapman, and after this missed cue kept hollering from the pit and pursing his lips in a kissing sound, "mwch, mwch, Chapaman, Chapaman!" After a very successful performance, a number of us singers restrained Bill Chapman from going to Basile's dressing room and strangling the conductor with his bare hands. So much for the marvelous rapport between foreign conductors and the American singer.

Leonard Bernstein: "It's As If I Dreamed It"

When your agent (God help me!) calls you up and tells you to get down to Carnegie Hall for an audition, you don't ask the "why or wherefore." You get yourself together and get down there at the right time and in the right voice.

Being a young opera singer in New York City without any *chutzpah*, I went to auditions not knowing who or what it was for. So I vocalized, got my music, took the Long Island Railroad (changing at Jamaica), ran onto the subway, and got off at the 59th Street station. Carnegie Hall was waiting. The acoustically wonderful, wide expanse of the hall was frightening from the stage where I now stood looking off into the blackness of a seemingly empty cavern of seats.

I had the accompanist play "*In diesen heil'gen Hallen*," the tried and true basso aria from Mozart's *The Magic Flute*. (I loved this aria for auditions. It showed off my low E at the end and it never went higher than I could sing.) There seemed to be no one in the hall as I sang my aria. I was in good voice and as I sang I thought, "Well, this is going pretty well." At most auditions I have been so frightened that I could barely get my voice going. My whole life has been being frightened. I remember trying to audition for the Met and having a filling fall out of one of my back teeth as I walked on the stage. This was a little different. No one seemed to be there.

But I was wrong. Down the stage-right aisle a swiftly moving figure was running towards the stage. Who was this frantic person? I had finished my aria, so perhaps it was a stage manager hurrying to throw me out. (As a 14-year-old, I had once been dismissed from the position as an usher at Chicago's Orchestra Hall, because I had snuck out and played the concert grand on the stage an hour before the performance. I pounded out my version of the Rachmaninoff *Prelude* that every kid knew back at my high school, but the orchestra's librarian was not impressed. He threw me out). So now I thought, "Here it comes again!"

Up onto the stage bounded Leonard Bernstein. I was shocked. The energetic conductor walked right up to me and face to face said, "It's like I dreamed it! You are Mathis!" I mumbled back, "Who is Mathis?" Lenny sat down at the piano and threw a large orchestra score for *Mathis der Maler* by Paul Hindemith onto the piano, and pointing at it said, "Sing some of this." I did and got the job. It's like I dreamed it.

Nadia Boulanger: Carissimi! It's a Forest Fire!

I have always wondered what studying with Nadia Boulanger would be like. She had taught many of my composer friends and, of course, many of America's finest composers (Aaron Copland, among others). But I had never thought I would be with her as a singer, following her downbeat, or following *her*, carrying her briefcase and trying to catch up with her on the New York State College campus in Potsdam, New York, while we rushed to a rehearsal of Carissimi's *Jephte*. But there I was, rushing after the tiny, 78-year-old, French Grand Teacher of many composers—Nadia Boulanger.

She had been invited by the outstanding professor of music, Helen Hosmer. Professor Hosmer, a longtime distinguished member of the Crane Music Faculty, was instrumental in bringing to Potsdam some of the world's outstanding musicians, among whom were Aaron Copland and Robert Shaw. There is, on the campus of SUNY at Potsdam, the Helen Hosmer Concert Hall in memory of this great music educator.

The closest I had ever come to Boulanger had been a few years before, singing her sister Lili's *Psalm 150* at the Washington Cathedral with the organist, conductor, and director of music at the National Cathedral, Paul Callaway. A beautiful work for chorus, soloists, and orchestra, the piece has a sarrusophone (a metallic bass clarinet) in the orchestration and, as the other work on the program also used a sarrusophone, Stravinsky's *Threni*, it seemed appropriate programming (although it took me 120 hours to learn the bass part in the Stravinsky, with its 12-tone unaccompanied canons for 5 voices.)

Nadia was the most efficient and quick little 78-year-old I had ever encountered.

She had these little *pince-nez* glasses on her nose when she was conducting and she looked like a little tiny beautiful French bird. But some of the young students, who were only used to an hour standing in rehearsal, would occasionally faint or quietly collapse before the end of her four-hour rehearsals. I had been able to interview her at one point in the time I was there and asked her about teaching. She told me quite simply that the most important thing was getting the composer-student to try always to make *la grande ligne* ("the long line") throughout whatever piece he or she was composing. She was one of the most efficient and clear conductors I have ever worked with and I would have suffered an earthquake or a forest fire to sing for her.

Some Others: Hither and Yon

Opera will not go away. It seems to have entered the collective minds of the American public and will continue to rest there as a part of our nineteenth-century European-influenced thinking. In the tiniest towns and hamlets and universities across the United States, opera will still raise its uncompromising, strange, and marvelous head. The combination of music and drama merged into a stage spectacle of one size or another still seems to keep re-emerging in the strangest of places. As of 2016, there were 109 active opera companies in the United States, not counting colleges and universities. I have been to a few.

I do not like to mention the exact small cities or towns—even hamlets—where I have performed opera, as these places have had some success with their productions despite monetary troubles and deserve to continue to grow without criticism from me. But let me tell of a few humorous—or not so humorous—encounters I have had without naming them specifically so as not to damage the hopeful, continuing good health of opera in these communities.

The conductor/producer/manager/set designer in one company was explaining to the principals of the cast his model set for the production of *Don Pasquale* by Donizetti. In doing so, he inadvertently touched the darling little model of the turntable he planned to have built for the set to be mounted upon, and the entire model fell to pieces on the spot. We all chuckled, a bit nervously, not knowing then how true to life the model would prove. And, in fact, during the first performance I was just finishing a recitative, when the set began rotating and the most horrendous noise of cracking and splintering wood reached my ears.

The set was falling to pieces! The conductor/producer/manager/ set designer, looking up horrified from the pit, was hollering, "Schtop, schtop! Cloze ze curtains." The young choristers who were at that same moment running out on the stage for their big comic number suddenly stopped and, with heads bowed in embarrassment, slowly went into the wings. The bewildered audience heard furious hammering and yelling behind the now closed curtains. I remembered the pre-performance introduction to our *Don Pasquale* by our conductor/producer/manager/ set designer and thought, "Ah yes! Another scene on the prairies of American Opera."

In a city at the southern-most part of our opera-going country, the company technicians had forgotten to cool the stage temperature (nearly 90 degrees) to match that of the auditorium. As the curtains opened for the first scene in Wagner's *Tannhäuser*, the chorus and I (playing Hermann, the Landgrave of Thuringia) were suddenly overpowered by the blasts of cold air from the audience. I'm not sure that either side of the footlights ever recovered from that experience.

In a midwestern city, I found myself in the midst of plastic-covered couches and chairs on the bare wooden floor of a high school in the first scene of another production of Donizetti's *Don Pasquale*. This time the stage director of the production had realized, a week before the opening, that he had forgotten to engage someone to sing the Notary role. So we did without him. This detail seemed to be overlooked by the young audience, and we went fumbling along through the show.

I was directing *The Rise and Fall of the City of Mahagonny* by Bertholt Brecht and the conductor of the orchestra, also producer/director/manager of the production, informed me that there was no money to hire a banjo player for the orchestral music. He wanted to use the spinet piano. This is impossible! I said I would personally pay for the banjo player. To have "O Moon of Alabama" sung without the proper cabaret music was just not going to happen. Making these kind of sacrifices for the sake of small town budgets drives me crazy. Why do the work in the first place? If you schedule a work, then do it the way it is supposed to be done—period. Damn the expenses.

Photographs

Herb Beattie, conducting at Buffalo, NY, 1958

Herb Beattie with Pablo Casals, Florida State University, 1964

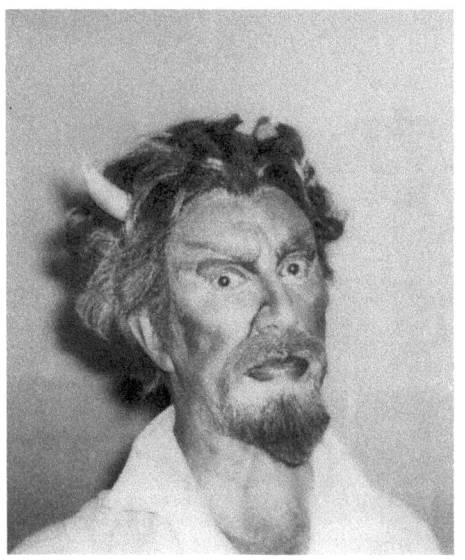

Faust, Lake George Opera Company, 1978

The Mikado, The Chicago Railroad Fair, 1951

Erismena, 1974, with soprano Carole Bogard

A Soldier's Tale, Colorado Opera Festival, 1972

Love for Three Oranges, Colorado Opera Festival, 1972

Abduction from the Seraglio, 1961

Italian Girl in Algiers, San Francisco, c.1960

King, in *Erismena*, Amsterdam, 1974 (top & bottom)

Leporello, *Don Giovanni*, Central City Opera, 1967 (top & bottom)

Leporello, *Don Giovanni*, Central City Opera, 1967

Don Pasquale, San Francisco, 1969

Osmin, *Abduction from the Seragalio*, 1961

Don Pasquale, San Francisco, 1972

Italian Girl in Algiers, San Francisco, c.1960 (top & bottom)

Italian Girl in Algiers, with Marilyn Horne, San Francisco, 1973

Italian Girl in Algiers, 1973

The Singers

THE SINGERS

Ritual Gestures and Nervous Habits

I have noticed over a number of years that singers often (like many of us) develop habits in their body movements when they are performing. We see it in sports—for example, a tennis player who, before he can serve, must go through certain routine movements with his body, hands, or feet. Often a pitcher on a professional baseball team will pull his hat, spit, or rub the ball around in his hand before delivering the pitch. I have even noticed that Olympic runners getting set before a race have a developed routine of doing certain things with their bodies or faces that help them relax or prepare for the second they begin the race. The same is apparent in singers. You'll notice certain singers (although taught not to do so) always moving their hands in a certain arc or beating time to the music with a foot or nodding head, sometimes clutching their fingers and moving their arms about strangely. Sometimes there are contortions of the face and mouth that can be dramatically off-putting to the audience. I see some singers who sing out of the sides of their mouths or have distinct and distracting chin wobbles. If they are far enough away from the audience—fine. But up close—say, on TV—*uh oh*!

But of all these habits, the worst in my opinion is the old-fashioned European way of running up to the footlights for the high note. This last can be particularly upsetting to an opera director who is simply trying to get some realism into the movement of the character the singer is portraying. I guess it was fine and expected in some old-fashioned, romantic operas years ago, but not today.

I was directing *The Rise and Fall of the City of Mahagonny* by Bertolt Brecht one summer in Colorado, and things were going well until we began rehearsals on stage. At the moment the brilliantly acting, vocally wonderful Greek contralto playing the role of the Widow Begbick came to her high note, she rushed from her position midstage to the footlights to sing the note and the final bars of the aria. I rushed to tackle her, thinking she was going to hurl herself into the orchestra pit and certain injury, but this was not the case. She told me she *had* to run to the front of the stage for this final high note of her aria as she had *always* seen it done that way and had *always* done it that way. It was difficult to convince her that in the modern theater, in America, one does not do these things. It is just simply ridiculous for the Widow Begbick at this point in the opera to become seized by an uncontrollable fit and rush to the footlights.

Not only was this true of that time in Colorado, but once a professional opera tenor insisted on jumping off the throne of the king in *Un ballo in maschera* by Verdi and rushing to the footlights for his big high note. In rehearsal (thank goodness!) this was caught in time, and after lots of working over and several football-type tackles, he was cured by opening night.

I am always amused when singers show up for rehearsals of an opera and insist that they have always done it "This Way" and "No Other Way Will Do." Considering the terrible, stagnant repertoire in today's opera schedules and the short period of time for rehearsals, leading touring opera singers end up having to do this. I have heard that in ancient days famous singers would have their friend, teacher, or wife simply pick out a costume for them to wear and—regardless of the staging—just walk in and knock the audience's ears off with their voices. I witnessed some singers in a Met staging of Wagner's Ring Cycle refuse to go near the machine that made sections of the set go up and down as it was grinding along on the stage. They were afraid of being ground up into opera singer sausage, I guess. One can see their point of view! And it's true, opera singing is not without its physical dangers. Falls and set malfunctions can take a toll on a performer's wellbeing. I remember wondering if my back would recover in time for a performance of C. W. Gluck's *Orpheus and Eurydice* after I caught our soprano, Maralin Niska, when she fell off a ladder during rehearsal. Sopranos, as a rule, need a lot of "relaxed weight" to deliver the goods in performance, and Maralin was no exception.

Well, finally, whether flying above the stage 100 feet in the air as a circus performer, or riding on an often poorly drugged horse, or suspended in a basket 45 feet in the air—for the performer it's really just a matter of the doing it, getting paid, and getting the next plane out of there. I, for one who has been involved many times, highly recommend these last habits.

Sopranos

The soprano voice is inhabited by a variety of types, temperaments, and shapes. Let me begin by discussing temperaments. This subject could be discussed much better in my mind by a range of psychiatrists and psychologists, rather than conductors, stage directors, and fellow singers, not to speak of managers and *intendants*.

But here are a few examples of soprano behavior I have witnessed.

What do you do with the lyric soprano who insists on upstaging you in a performance of Rossini's *Italian Girl in Algiers* in a prominent West Coast opera house production by wiggling and shaking her butinsky behind you as you are trying to sing a long solo aria? Answer: Kick her in the shins.

When a leading Wagnerian dramatic soprano with an unusually large and frightening set of mammaries suggests to you during the after-opera dinner cocktail celebration at the singers' table that she wants to "fick you," what do you say?

It's just a matter of simple physics, of course, that sopranos generally need a certain amount of corpulence to project their voices, and frequently this is "up front." Such was the case with the marvelous soprano Carole Bogard, who sang the part of the slave girl Aldimira opposite my King Erimante in a 1974 production of Francesco Cavalli's *Erismena* in Amsterdam. Our puckish director, Alan Curtis, had Aldimira kneel in front of me as I sat on my throne and, in a gesture of desperate entreaty, pull my head down into her boundless cleavage. Upon resurfacing, I was to sing the words "Command me!" I had no trouble effecting the dazed wonder I was supposed to project after this encounter. The audience loved it.

Okay. It's dress rehearsal and the rented set from Miami is too large for your stage. The soprano has learned to be a prima donna overnight, so almost anything can upset her and you forgot to tell her about that set from Miami that is too large for the stage and you've got to cut down on set changes or the audience will be sitting out there all night looking at a closed curtain. Well, she looks up, and guess what? The tenor is not walking down a staircase for their big duet. He just walks out at stage level and steps up on the platform. In a loud, menacing voice she says "Where are the steps the tenor is supposed to walk down to me on for this scene?"

Suddenly you feel terribly tired. You know you should have said something to her about that huge staircase being left in the wings so we didn't have to take the time to move it with our small band of stagehands. The soprano bursts into tears. She can't continue with the rehearsal. You look around for help, but everyone has left you, even the tenor. So you start to try to explain, but instead you are rushing backstage following the soprano to her dressing room. She's crying harder and starting to go into a kind of mild hysterics. What do you do? You reach for the Kleenex and with the other arm you hold the weeping prima donna. After three to five minutes when the sobbing quiets down, you start to explain, hoping against hope that this will put the diva's nerves back in place and we can resume the rehearsal. It worked!

Lee Venora: The Soprano Who Peed Her Pants

Not all sopranos are giants. In San Francisco I was playing the fat banker, Don Iñigo Gomez, in Ravel's beautiful one-act opera *L'heure espagnole*. We were rehearsing in a small, rather garage-looking place in the North Beach. The baritone playing the Muleteer was Richard Fredricks. He was annoyed that the lovely petite soprano, Lee Venora (playing Concepción), had brought along to the rehearsal her new pet dog. A scraggly-looking, mid-sized hound, it went unleashed and roaming around the room, peeing on the floor, jumping up on Venora, and wanting to be petted or fed or something. Fredricks kept cursing Venora and her dog and finally gave up. The antagonism between the baritone and the soprano was too much, and the rehearsal was cancelled.

Several weeks later there was a rehearsal on stage with the set and props for the opera. Fredricks was urged by the stage manager to practice picking up and carrying the tall, empty grandfather clock that stood on the set up the stairs to Concepción's bedroom to see if he could do it comfortably. As the Muleteer, he needed to portray a young and virile man who was powerful enough to carry the clock.

The clock had a false back, so that the other two characters (would-be lovers of Concepción, the Banker and the Poet) could easily slip in and out of it, leaving the clock empty and therefore easy for Fredricks to hoist on his shoulders and carry upstairs to Concepción's bedroom. However, in this piano dress rehearsal, this is not what happened. Fredricks (always a very self-assured artist) told the stage manager not to worry—lifting the clock would be *no problem*. Fredricks's scene with the clock arrived, and all on stage watched the baritone reach down, pick up the clock, and then lose his hold and, twisting around, let the whole thing drop to his feet.

There was a sudden surprised gasp by all except Lee Venora, who let out a screaming howl of laughter and went running off the stage, peeing in her pants. The rehearsal continued later without a hitch, with a chagrined Muleteer and a comfortably redressed Concepción. Lesson: Always do what the stage manager tells you.

Butterfly: The Foot-in-Mouth Routine

I had been singing one of the roles in opera I hate most one summer in Central City, Colorado. There are a lot of these *comprimario* (supporting) roles for basses, such as the Baron in *Traviata*, the Landlord in *Bohème*, or the Ghost of Hector in Berlioz's *Les Troyens*. But the Bonze in Puccini's *Madame Butterfly* has to be the worst! You are bald headed with the very unstable shoes to which I have already alluded. If the set is designed—as it was in Central City—by the terrific set designer Robert O'Hearn, then you must be able to navigate quickly on these precarious platforms through a little pond of water on a walkway of rocks. It's beautiful, but dangerous. One misstep or trip will ruin you and the set. I had to do the part, as it was important to have singers do several roles in the Central City Opera Festival, from leading roles to small ones.

However, this opera must have a Butterfly who can sing the role with a beautiful lyric voice and display a talent for dramatic roles. The problem at Central City was that—although she acted and sang the role beautifully—the soprano was not the diminutive figure needed to *look* right in the role—far from it! (The ushers that season had done a parody on the show and called their version *Madame Butterball*.)

To get to the point, I was later that season in New York, auditioning for Sarah Caldwell and the Opera Company of Boston. Miss Caldwell, in all her corpulent fullness sitting before me, asked how the set was in Central City's production that summer. I went into rapturous details about O'Hearn's set but then, after my description, added that the Butterfly doing the role was outstanding vocally and acting-wise, but on that tiny beautiful set was way *too large* a girl. "In fact, she was just too *fa*—." I quickly shut my mouth, but I had already put my foot in it (Japanese footwear or not) up to the shoe laces. I can still see the frown on Sarah's face. But she realized almost immediately that the person she was auditioning was just a singer, and a bass at that, so what could one expect? She hired me anyway, foot in mouth and all.

Tenors

I suppose it is a welcome—or perhaps unwelcome—set of genes that causes an otherwise normal human to be born a "tenor." (Note: *Not* a countertenor. That is something wildly different!) Let's say the high register of the middle voice in its top range. Say, above an A in the treble clef and upwards to high C and perhaps even E above that. The tenor voice is just about as thrilling as the dramatic soprano in the high register. Listening to Björling, Di Stefano, Gigli, or Pavarotti singing at their best—high notes, legato line, or just the drama of those voices—is beyond question one of the great thrills in the vocal literature. It is a dangerous task for a singer to reach the very high notes without cracking. Knowing that you are being paid to sing those high notes, knowing that the audience is going to give up screaming applause for it—it's very similar to a high-wire act in the circus. If you make it, success; if not, tremendous failure.

But what about those tenors one has worked with and found sometimes a bit lacking in the upper story, if not the upper voice? Let me mention a few I have known.

At the old City Center on 55th Street in New York, a tenor having just completed a rehearsal on stage dragged me back to his dressing room and—ending up just above the latrine—insisted that I look at the phlegm he was spitting from his mouth. He kept crying out to me, "Look! It's a green-yellow color!" I got away as soon as I could.

Talking about throat crazies: One tenor came to performances with a box filled with what looked like surgical instruments, all shiny and laid out in their satin beds. He did not illustrate for me how they were used, but I presumed they were stuck into the mouth and throat and then expanded so the singer could easily look down (with a mirror) into the area of the vocal chords and check to see if the chords were in good condition.

What about costumes and tenors? I was told by one tenor that he could not sing high C unless he wore his own special boots. The costumer, a very obliging young lady, said, "But he can't wear those boots as the Caliph in *Turandot*. It just wouldn't look right." I confronted the singer, and he said, "Well, I can't sing high C unless I wear my boots." I knew the audience would prefer the high C over the proper footwear for a caliph, so I said okay. He wore them and, yes, he did sing high C. By the way, don't ever ask a tenor to wear a hat. After one second on the stage, he will take it off so the audience can see his fine mop of hair.

One tenor singing the Messenger in an *Aida* concert performance showed up in a full cutaway tuxedo. One tenor singing Radamès in the same opera wore a blue suit and blue suede shoes and a *Saturday Night Live* hairpiece at the Sunday afternoon performance. The baritone dressed in a tight-fitting tux and looked like George Raft, an American film actor known for playing gangsters, and both the ladies singing Aida and Amneris wore very large fur coats.

Of course, some tenors (only a few) may object to the Don Pasquale in the Donizetti opera using a spray gun and spraying the flowers on the set while he is singing his aria in Act 1.

Then there was the tenor, Michele Molese, who spoke directly to the music critic after he had finished his big aria in *Faust* at the New York City Center: "That pinched high C was for you, Mr. Schonberg." The stunt cost him his job.

I know from hearing stories from the old City Center days that the tenor David Poleri got so mad at the tempo that the conductor, Joseph Rosenstock, was taking in the final scene in *Carmen* that he walked off the stage and let the Carmen commit suicide. I understand David would often take off his shoes during a recital. I guess he was more comfortable that way.

I even saw a leading tenor at the Met, in a *Turandot* performance, spit to his side before singing his aria. Interesting staging, I must say.

One friend of mine, a French Canadian tenor, refused to kiss the soprano in the opera *Romeo and Juliet*. I guess he was afraid she might have a cold. It seemed kind of strange for Romeo not to kiss Juliet at any time during the opera.

Another tenor artist singing the part of the Narrator in the Bach *St. Mathew Passion* sang "And Jesus, I mean Peter, went into the..." The Washington, D.C., National Cathedral audience didn't seem to mind. I wondered about this change of text.

The lyric tenor Frank Porretta leaned over to me and in a whisper said his zipper was wide open. I assured him, as we sat in front of the Friday afternoon concert audience in the Academy of Music in Philadelphia with Eugene Ormandy and the Philadelphia Symphony, that there was little I could do about it. As the maestro raised his baton, Frank walked quickly off stage and just as quickly returned onstage to sing beautifully his part in *The Childhood of Christ* by Hector Berlioz. At intermission, Ormandy asked us quizzically what had happened. We told him, and he laughed and reminded us, before we walked back on the stage for the second part of the concert, "to always the check our flys."

Joaquin Romaguera, one of my favorite tenors, had me up to dinner one night in his apartment in New York City. Things were great, the food was wonderful, the company excellent, when Joaquin asked me to go over to the freezer and take out a package of frozen butter. I opened the lid of the freezer and found on the top of the food the plastic bag holding the body of the Romagueras' frozen dead cat.

Baritones

Baritones are usually the hardest to get to follow your stage direction. The reason is that they are often smarter than you are. In any number of opera performances I have learned from baritones what I can do to make my role as singer or stage director much better. There are a few exceptions however.

In Duluth, Minnesota, I was called to come up from New York and stage *Un ballo in maschera*. It is an opera I have had little to do with in my career, as there is not much, if any, comedy in it and the only bass roles are a couple of hopeless idiots whom one would not put on one's resume. Anyway, in the case of the Duluth Minnesota Opera, the baritone was the inimitable Russian Igor Gorin. What a privilege to work with him! A golden voice that I can think of as being rivaled only by Robert Merrill's. He had never been cast in *Ballo*, so he was a bit concerned about what to do at the close of the aria "*Eri tu*." I didn't have an idea in the world what to tell him until I saw the picture of the king hanging over the fireplace. It suddenly came to me: Why doesn't the aria end with the baritone toasting the king with a champagne glass and then throwing the glass into the fireplace? Little did I realize the time it would take to work on this bit of staging.

At first Igor decided he didn't like it and what was more, his wife didn't like it. So I forgot about the idea and went back to my hotel to get a good night's sleep. At 1 a.m. the phone rang. It was Igor saying that he had thought it over and he and his wife thought it might just work. Could I come early for the next day's rehearsal and try it out with him? I said (foolishly), "Of course." At 9:30 a.m. we were on stage with the champagne glass and a couple of chairs lined up as a fireplace and Gorin's wife on the sidelines (all starring, great male singers seem to have their respective wives standing or sitting by during rehearsals to make sure their darling boys are not badly treated) waiting to pounce if something seemed wrong. I was very, very, careful. I demonstrated the throwing of the glass. Gorin worked with me and seemed delighted, but wanted to rehearse this bit over and over. In fact, five days of this early rehearsing of the glass-at-the-portrait-into-the-fireplace was urging me closer and closer to complete hysteria. At one point, early on in the rehearsals, the glass (plastic, of course) bounced out of the fireplace and jumped playfully about on the floor of the stage, and I thought the whole idea was finished. But no, Gorin's wife came to the rescue and chastised her husband for not doing it right and not being a good artist. We continued, and I got closer and closer to madness. Finally it worked. On opening night, Igor Gorin threw the glass he had toasted with at the king's picture perfectly straight into the fireplace and sang a wonderful ringing high note. All the work on that bit probably was worth it, but I thought I'd better be careful in the future of my career as an opera stage director to ask for something extra. Just take what they have and let them alone. After all, the only thing the conductor, producer, and audience really want is great singing. Igor Gorin did that *and* threw the glass after the high note. Everyone applauded—even his wife.

Basses

I remember singing my first recital when I was 15 at the American Conservatory of Music. John C. Wilcox, my teacher, had me singing "Rolling Down to Rio," a particularly old concert favorite of the recital repertory in the early twentieth century. It's a typical nineteenth-century song without much to recommend it except that the high notes were within range for a young bass and its jolly humor made it about right for the young singer.

I got through most of it but cracked on the high note at the end of the song. Very depressing for me, and I turned after the meager applause and got off the stage as quickly as possible. But Wilcox grabbed me by the arm and led me back on stage. He explained that he thought I could do much better singing this song and told me and the audience that I would sing the whole song again.

You might imagine how I felt. If there had been any way of escaping this terrible embarrassment I would have found it. But, alas, no such choice presented itself to me in that paralyzing moment. So I did as I was told and sang the song again and cracked again on the high note.

Later, in his studio, Wilcox told me he did it to teach me a fundamental problem I must overcome. Not Practicing Enough! I did just that after that lesson but always was worried about high notes. So much for the bass voice or should I say "bass mind."

Fishing in Kodiak, Alaska

I thought my recital tour for Alaskan Music Trails was going along well until my accompanist and I found ourselves in the fishing village of Kodiak. The first bad sign was the pair of very dusty curtains in the small hall where we were performing. In fact, they produced a dust screen that partly enveloped the stage and the audience when drawn open. However, the real shock came when I was introduced as a "bass," with a short "a" like the fish. I complied by doing a breaststroke movement and opening and closing my mouth like a fish as I walked on the stage. I wondered what kind of bass I was: small-mouth, big-mouth, or sea bass? I did get some nice applause from the audience before singing a note, as at least some of them got the joke.

The Tinkling Commendatore

I was directing *Don Giovanni* in Colorado Springs and decided that the singer in the role of the Commendatore needed a louder voice. The quality of his voice was beautiful but the quantity had to be much more for the final scene. I decided we would use a personal throat microphone on the singer to amplify his voice. It was amusing and somewhat puzzling to hear the tinkling of fluid and then flushing of water during Zerlina's aria on stage. Apparently the Commendatore had forgotten to turn off his mic when relieving himself in the washroom. Ah, modern sound systems! How wonderful and unexpected they can be!

A Very Sleepy Finale

Doing children's concerts is usually a lot of fun, except when you agree to sing too many on tour. I was so pleased when the rolypoly (in her ermine coat) bank president's wife in Fairbanks, Alaska, asked me to do an extra children's concert. I was exhausted at the end of the tour, but thought, "Ah, another piece of money! I'll do it." The gym I was singing in was perfect for the school, but not necessarily for singing. The room was circular and the roof twirled up to a kind of point with the whole thing reminding me of an ice cream cone. My last song was "Sailormen," made famous by the baritone John Charles Thomas. The ending of the song has the singer going to sleep with the words "and I am as sleepy as . . . (yawn) . . . John." The singer yawns and closes his eyes and pretends to fall asleep as he sings this last phrase. However, in this case, I was so tired I actually did fall asleep and sank to my knees. My accompanist rushed over to pick me up, thinking I had fainted or had a heart attack. I awoke to the best applause I had ever had with this song from the young audience and no one had realized I had fallen asleep except me and my accompanist. So much for reality on the children's circuit.

Favorite Fellows

My favorite bass singer and actor was Norman Treigle. A sensational voice mixed with an electricity on the stage, he blew audiences out of their seats with his singing and acting. More than that, he was a pleasure to work with. We used to laugh about our "deviated septums." Norman was also a gracious colleague. He once brought me down stage to share in a standing ovation that rightfully was for him as the more major role. Julius Rudel himself often told the story of his "perfect" *Don Giovanni* with Treigle as the Don and me as Leporello. I'm sure I deserved this designation partly because those two greats had helped draw out the best I had to offer.

Another favorite fellow bass of mine was Arnold Voketaitis. He was fun to be around off stage, and it was inspiring to share the stage with him. At one performance of *The Barber of Seville* in San Antonio, Arnold and I got better reviews than Beverly Sills, whose star power was responsible for the packed audience.

Other Characters

OTHER CHARACTERS

Strange Students

The Corman sisters seemed harmless enough young ladies at the University of Buffalo, in Rochester, New York. They were voice students, but were more interested in the stage; hence, they showed up at the opera workshop. I was somewhat good-natured at that time in my teaching career, and so if students such as they persuaded me to come home to meet their families and experience an unusual evening of spiritual enlightenment, chances are that I would accept—provided my wife or a fellow faculty member of the Music Department came along. In this case, I asked a new friend of mine on the faculty, Livingston Gearhart. He was a metropolitan fellow and graduate of the Paris Music School, in addition to being a terrific arranger of choral pieces, a chain smoker, and surefooted piano accompanist. He also collected pieces of glass that he said came from outer space.

The night we decided to go was in late January. It was Buffalo City cold, and a wind from the lake was blowing that always meant to turn up one's collar and get inside as soon as possible.

The Corman sisters lived in an old section of town that ran to just about every kind of spooky-looking building you could think of. Two stories of rickety wood, dreary paint, and a walk up the long front stairs to an ancient door that was difficult to see did not exactly seem welcoming.

Gearhart and I had been laughing earlier that day about ghosts and specters and spiritualism. We thought we were sophisticated young university ideologues who stuck out like sore thumbs in this old city, a northern city of steel workers dominated by immigrants and less-than-urban minds. We were terribly sure we knew, if not all the answers, then most of them. And things that go bump in the night were not among the things we had determined could exist. I had apparently long ago dismissed an earlier encounter with the supernatural. My first serious girlfriend (I even gave her a ring!) had claimed to be a spiritualist, though that was not what I found most interesting about her at the time. One day, not long after her mother had died, I was at her home and we were making out pretty heavily on a couch in the living room. Suddenly a lampshade detached itself from a lamp and flew across the room in front of us. "That's just Mother," she said. Oddly enough, the prospect of having a ghost for a mother-in-law was not the reason I later broke up with her. No, it was a far more prosaic reason: I had found a new love in the distant city where I was studying at the time.

Anyway, flash forward a decade. Janey Corman invited us into her somewhat rustic-looking living room, and seated in a circle were her father and mother and her older sister, Janelle. They welcomed us as if we were going to church and then suggested that we all sing a hymn. The worn and tattered hymn books were on each chair and we opened them and sang a tired old hymn with tired airy voices.

After the hymn, Janelle leaned back in her chair, opened her mouth, and began gasping and gurgling, shaking her head. The voice that came from her mouth was not hers. It was somewhat British in its dialect and rather high. Certainly not her voice. Her sister in a reassuring tone quickly said, "That's her guide."

I looked around the room and Gearhart was not laughing. No one was laughing. In fact, we all were staring at Janelle. I thought her father might collapse, but he seemed perfectly calm (although white as a sheet), and with a slight smile. Janelle's guide was short of breath and very soft. He said, "I'm with you, Janelle, so don't be frightened. Just remember to always be confident and unafraid." There was more, but I can't remember it. I know that Gearhart and I and our wives left soon after this experience and did not laugh or think the evening was funny in any way. So goes our involvement with the Corman sisters. In other words, don't take your opera singer students for granted.

The Agent

Ludwig Lustig was a huge, heavy man of German heritage. He was seemingly not an expert of opera singers, but he seemed to know a lot about voices. He whispered when he talked on the phone to you. And he often projected bad or good news—mostly bad.

But again, he would often place you in his mind as a certain category of singer. For me, it was difficult, because he knew I could always be a character bass in opera. So he always typecast me in comic roles, such as Dr. Bartolo in *The Barber of Seville*. It was a character role that I excelled in doing. I had a natural comic timing when I did these parts on the New York City Opera stage, as well as others. The upshot was that when an opera director called from out of town, he asked Lustig for a certain type of singer. Lustig immediately thought of me to fulfil these comic roles.

Lustig was not inclined to take "no" for an answer. Once, when I was in the North Shore Hospital with tubes sticking out most of my orifices, I received a call from Lustig. Upon learning of my condition, Lustig replied, "Other than that, Beattie, you will sing on Friday night." He wanted his $10 commission that I would generate by singing this role.

Often an out-of-town director would ask for a serious singer. But Lustig never considered me for such roles. He thought of me as a character singer, such as Bartolo in *Barber of Seville* or Don Pasquale in *Don Pasquale*, Mustafa in *The Italian Girl in Algiers*, or Osmin in *The Abduction from the Seraglio*. It irked me because I could sing serious roles in other operas because of my vocal ability. I had a large part of my career singing in oratorios with Eugene Ormandy, Robert Shaw, and William Steinberg. Thus, I was often frustrated by Lustig's insistence on characterizing me as a comic bass.

Lustig and I used to perform a little unspoken ritual whenever we had lunch together. The waiter would bring the check and usually set it down between us. After a time Lustig's hand would start to creep toward it. However, this creeping was glacially slow and I would eventually realize that if I had any hope to engage in any other activities that day I would have to step in and pay it. So invariably I would swoop in and grab the tab while Lustig threw his hands in the air with a surprised interjection along the lines of "Oh, my!"

The Makeup Artist

"Especially good myakup. . . . The rest stinks." These were the only words spoken to me by Michael Arshanky when we were watching a dress rehearsal of Puccini's great opera *Turandot* at the old City Center in 1958. Arshansky had (of course) done the makeup, as he was the main makeup man for the New York City Opera. No shortage of ego there.

Arshansky was a Russian who had trained as a ballet dancer and had a close association with Balanchine even before the two of them emigrated to the United States. He also had a talent for makeup, hence his job with the NYCO. He used to say to me, "Don't you make face, Beattie. I make face." And the more cryptic pronouncement that, "You have dead nose. I make you live nose." I can also still hear him saying with a wink in his eye as he strode into the chorus girls' dressing room: "Close eyes, girls! I'm coming in to do your myakup!"

On one memorable occasion when we were doing *Madame Butterfly* in Central City, Colorado, the tenor who was playing Pinkerton and I spent the summer morning fishing in Grand Lake not far away. As a result, when the tenor showed up for duty that evening he sported a flaming red sunburn. This somehow incensed Arshansky, who refused to make him up for his role. "You are no artist! You myakup your own face!" Arshansky said heatedly, as the tenor left the room, angrily banging the door behind him.

About the Author

Herbert Beattie is a world-renowned operatic bass, a conductor and director of opera, a professor of music, and a composer.

Herbert Beattie was born in Chicago in 1926 to Irish immigrants. His calling was clear almost from the start when, as a baby, he was often heard humming to himself in his stroller. By elementary school he was already performing musical numbers for his classmates. At the age of thirteen he won a scholarship to study voice at the American Conservatory of Music (then in Chicago). He was the youngest person ever to do so.

With World War II raging, Beattie enlisted in the Navy right after finishing high school and was sent to Arkansas for training. While there he organized and led a naval choir that toured the country. He also published a volume of poetry cowritten with his English teacher.

After the war, Beattie attended the University of Louisville in Kentucky through his sophomore year. He transferred to the Colorado College in Colorado Springs to finish his Bachelor of Arts degree. He continued studies at the famous Westminster Choir College in Princeton, New Jersey, for a graduate degree. Intending to become a teacher, Herb sought and was hired for a position on the music faculty of Syracuse University in upstate New York. From there he moved on to Pennsylvania State University and after a few years was hired to start the music program at the University of Buffalo. While there he was sent for training to be a conductor in Austria where a chance to sing the bass aria for the Mozart opera *The Abduction from the Seraglio* brought him such notice and praise that he was encouraged to switch to singing as a career. And so, a few years later, Beattie found himself engaged as a regular singer for the New York City Opera. He continued teaching, however, this time at Hofstra University on Long Island.

During his career, Herbert Beattie has sung virtually all major roles for an operatic bass, from pre-classical works to contemporary, including some of his own compositions. He has appeared in the storied opera halls of Europe doing the heavy lifting in classic and contemporary roles, to school gymnasiums in Alaska where he has delighted children of all ages with old and new popular fare. Herb is devoted to opening up the magic world of music for young people, and his affection for them is reciprocated. In the early 1990s he collaborated with the Colorado Springs Children's Choral to produce an opera he wrote called *The Operatic Attic*. Many of the child performers regularly came early to rehearsals to talk with Herb about music.

Opera companies throughout the United States have engaged Beattie to sing and/or direct, including ones in New York City, San Francisco, Boston, Dayton, Cincinnati, Louisville, Houston, Central City (Colorado), Denver, Miami, Fort Worth, Shreveport, St. Paul, and New Orleans. International engagements for Beattie have included performances in Vancouver, Toronto, Tel Aviv, Amsterdam, Brussels, and Rome.

Beattie has also maintained an active recital and concert career, performing with composers and conductors such as Darius Milhaud, Aaron Copland, William Walton, Benjamin Britten, Carlo Menotti, Pablo Casals, Carlisle Floyd, and Carlton Gamer. He has sung under the baton of John Finley Williamson, Joseph Krips, Leonard Bernstein, Nadia Boulanger, Zubin Mehta, Leopold Stokowski, Robert Shaw, Eugene Ormandy, William Steinberg, Donald Jenkins, Emerson Buckley, and Julius Rudel, among others.

From 1970 to 2000, Beattie was stage director and artist/singer for the Colorado Opera Festival, held annually in Colorado Springs, Colorado, under the auspices of the Colorado College and later an independent organization. He also sang bass roles in many oratorios and concerts produced by the Colorado College and the Colorado Springs Chorale under the direction of Donald P. Jenkins. Well into his eighties, Herbert Beattie was giving solo recitals to overflow crowds in his home town.

Herbert Beattie has been called a "singer's singer" but he also connects superbly with the concert-going public. Reviewers have been lavish in their praise. Some samples:

> [Herbert Beattie] ... acted in a neat comic style. He was a special hit with the audience. There was the customarily droll and finely sung Osmin of Herbert Beattie.
> —*The New York Times*

> As for Mr. Beattie, that fine singing-actor of the New York City Opera, he could no more sing in a concert opera without acting than—well, sing.
> —*New York Herald Tribune*

[Herbert Beattie] . . . is the perfect Leporello, ineffably funny without being an oaf or a clown—and more important; without tampering with the beauty of the basso's vocal part.

Beattie's Mustapha, just like his Osmin and Leporello, is a full-colored and enormously entertaining fellow . . . none more limber from the high G to low E or more versatile in tone from that of braggadocio romantic to buffoon."

—*San Francisco Chronicle*

The incomparable Herbert Beattie . . . his bottom tones cut through the night air like a bassoon.

Not only does [Herbert Beattie] sing beautifully . . . but mugs to perfection. And with taste.

—*San Francisco Examiner*

[Herbert Beattie] . . . quite simply stole the show.

—*Seattle Post*

While Herb is well-known for his singing, his more than 30-year career as a music educator has been every bit as important to him. He has had the honor and delight of mentoring many talented students beginning with his tenure teaching at Syracuse University, and then progressing to Pennsylvania State, the University of Buffalo, and Hofstra University on Long Island. Herbert Beattie received an honorary doctorate from the Colorado College in Colorado Springs in 1976. Many voice students have benefitted from private instruction from Herb throughout his career.

In addition to his musical endeavors, Beattie provided the authoritative voice-over for countless broadcast advertisements in the Front Range region of Colorado for over 30 years as voice talent for the Graham Advertising Agency in Colorado Springs. Herb came to be known as the "voice of God" both in advertisements and on the theatrical stage for a local production of *The Mystery Plays* adapted by Murray Ross at TheatreWorks in Colorado Springs in 1996.

Herbert Beattie resides in Colorado Springs with his wife Laurie and numerous feline companions. Beattie has five children and five grandchildren, and three great-grandchildren.

APPENDIX

The following are short biographical sketches of the people whom Herb encountered and mentioned in the text, compiled by the editor.

Kurt Herbert Adler (1905–1988)
Opera conductor.
Adler already had an extensive career in Europe when he was forced to leave by the Nazis in 1938. He landed with the San Francisco Opera in 1943 as chorus director. Ten years later he took over as general director, which position he held until 1981. Adler built the SFO into a world-class company with an expanded season. He sought out up-and-coming new singing talent, introducing such stars as Leontyne Price and Marilyn Horne and bringing European legends such as Birgit Nilsson and Elisabeth Schwarzkopf to the United States for the first time. He also nurtured new opera directors, and was known for encouraging innovative stage direction (which seems at odds with Herb's experience with him). Adler was known for being autocratic, uncompromising, and demanding of those he directed.

Peter Herman Adler (1899–1990)

Orchestral and opera conductor.

Born in what is now the Czech republic and forced to emigrate to the United States in 1939 after the rise of nazism, this conductor was best known for leading the NBC Opera Orchestra from 1950 to 1964 and the Baltimore Symphony Orchestra from 1959 to 1968. He was in demand as a guest conductor nationwide as well. Adler commissioned many new operas and pioneered the televised broadcast of classical music performances. Among the works that Adler commissioned are Menotti's *Amahl and the Night Visitors*, which has entered the popular repertoire as Christmas time fare. Adler was director of the American Opera Center at the Julliard School from 1973 until his retirement in 1981.

Victor Alessandro (1915–1976)

Opera conductor.

Alessandro was born in Texas to a prominent local conductor and music teacher. He attended the Eastman School of Music in Rochester, New York, and then trained in Europe at the Mozarteum in Salzburg and Saint Cecilia Academy in Rome. He returned to the United States and became conductor of the Oklahoma Symphony Orchestra in 1938. In 1950 he took over conducting the San Antonio Symphony, a post he held until 1975.

Michael Arshansky (1895–1978)

Makeup artist, actor, and dancer.

Arshansky was born in Moscow and joined the Moscow Art Theater as an actor. He studied dance and developed a close relationship with the choreographer George Balanchine while both were still in Russia. After emigrating, Arshansky danced with the Metropolitan Opera Ballet and at Radio City Music Hall in New York. He went to California in the 1930s where he reconnected with Balanchine, who cast him as a dancer in films such as *The Wizard of Oz*. Back in New York in the 1950s, Arshansky became the chief makeup artist for the Metropolitan Opera and the City Ballet. He continued his dance career and created the role of Drosselmeyer, the magician, in Balanchine's production of *The Nutcracker* in 1954.

Arturo Basile (1914–1968)
Italian opera conductor.
Basile was born in Sicily. He started out as an oboist, but switched to conducting after graduation from the Giuseppe Verdi Conservatory in Turin, Italy. In 1946 he won a prestigious conducting prize in Italy and his career took off. He eventually conducted at most of the world's major opera houses and he was in demand as a conductor for recordings. Basile is known mostly for Italian repertory, especially Puccini and Verdi. Tragically, his ascendant international career was cut short by his untimely death in an auto accident.

Leonard Bernstein (1918–1990)
One of the preeminent American conductors and composers of the twentieth century, Bernstein was also a pianist, author, and lecturer. As a conductor, he was most closely associated with the New York Philharmonic Orchestra, which he led from 1958 to 1969. However, he conducted most of the world's great orchestras and some not so great at one time or another. As a com-

poser, he is best known for his scores for the opera *Candide*, and the musical *West Side Story*. But he also wrote two other operas and several musicals; many orchestral works, including three symphonies; choral and vocal music; incidental music for other theater works; film scores; ballet music; chamber music for various ensembles; and music for solo piano. He lectured widely at many universities and colleges and was one of the first musicians to make use of television to educate the public, starting in 1954 and continuing until his death.

Carole Bogard (1936 –)

American soprano. Born in Cincinnati, Bogard studied music at the University of California at Berkeley, where she became a force in the movement to revive early vocal works in an authentic fashion. Bogard first came into prominence performing the title role in Handel's *Semele* at the forgotten work's American premiere in 1959, which took place at the Ravinia Festival near Chicago. Soon she was in demand internationally for her special talents bringing Baroque styles back to life. She sang regularly with the Amsterdam Opera and early music and chamber music ensembles throughout the United States. A versatile stylist with impeccable musical instincts, Bogard was also a sought-after star for the more standard operatic repertory, from Mozart to Strauss. She is also known for bringing contemporary American works to the public. She has recorded the major song cycles of Aaron Copland and Ned Rorem, but has also championed the works of lesser known American vocal composers such as John Alden Carpenter, William Flanagan, John Duke, and Richard Cumming.

Lili Boulanger (1893–1918)

French composer.

Boulanger, the daughter of two musicians, was a child prodigy who started music theory lessons at the Paris Conservatoire before the age of ten. She played numerous instruments, including piano, organ, violin, cello, and harp. Lili won the Prix de Rome for composition in 1913, the first woman to do so. Always sickly, Lili died of intestinal tuberculosis at the age of 24. She left numerous vocal and orchestral works and an unfinished opera. She was the younger sister of Nadia Boulanger.

Nadia Boulanger (1887–1979)

French music teacher, conductor, and composer.

Nadia was a child prodigy who studied at the Paris Conservatoire and won or nearly won several illustrious composition prizes. However, as money issues became pressing for her family, she concentrated on teaching as a source of income. Many twentieth-century American composers studied with her over the years. She also had an active conducting career, being the first woman to conduct both the London Philharmonic and the Boston Symphony Orchestra. She taught music at many ivy league American colleges during World War II, when she resided in the United States. Returning to Paris after the war, Boulanger taught private students in her family apartment until her death, while maintaining an active schedule as lecturer and conductor all over the world.

Emerson Buckley (1914–1989)

Opera conductor.

Born in New York City and educated at Columbia University,

Buckley began conducting in 1936, first with the Columbia Grand Opera, then with the Mutual Broadcasting System's orchestra. He was the music director and resident conductor for the Greater Miami Opera from 1950 to 1986. Buckley was widely sought after as a guest conductor and praised for his artistry and ability to mount productions quickly. For the New York City Opera, he conducted the premieres of both Douglas Moore's opera *The Ballad of Baby Doe*, and Robert Ward's *The Crucible*. In later years he toured extensively with the tenor Luciano Pavarotti, conducting the local orchestras that accompanied him.

Sarah Caldwell (1924–2006)

American opera director, producer, and conductor.

Caldwell was a child prodigy violinist. By the age of 23 she had staged her first opera, Vaughn Williams's one-act *Riders to the Sea*, and her future course was set. In 1952 she became head of the Boston University Opera Workshop and five years later founded an opera company that later became the Opera Company of Boston. Here she became known for taking chances on difficult and underperformed operas, and also for creative and unusual staging of the standard operatic fare. Caldwell was famously corpulent, a fact that figured in Herb's encounter with her.

Paul Callaway (1909–1995)

American organist and choral conductor.

He was the organist and choirmaster at the Washington National Cathedral in Washington, D.C., from 1939 to 1977. Callaway was also active in opera, founding in 1956 what is now known as the Washington National Opera.

Alan Curtis (1934 – 2015)

Opera conductor, musicologist, and harpsichordist.

Alan Curtis was born in Mason, Michigan, and displayed musical talent at the keyboard from an early age. He took a liking to the sound of early instruments and received a Fulbright scholarship to study the harpsichord in Amsterdam in 1957. In 1960 he joined the faculty of the music school at the University of California at Berkeley, where he helped propel the early music movement and championed the idea of using authentic period instruments and ensembles for Baroque works, instead of the overwrought and opulent arrangements for these pieces that had become the norm. Curtis turned his attention to opera and soon was conducting forgotten Baroque classics at Berkeley and other U.S. venues. Perhaps to be closer to his subject, Curtis lived in Italy starting in the 1970s and became a sought-after director of Baroque opera on the European continent for the next 20 years. He also revived several extinct early musical instruments and collaborated on a project to record 12 formerly unknown songs about animals by George Frideric Handel, entitled *Handel's Bestiary*.

Marta Casals Istomin (1936–) (née Marta Montáñez y Martínez)

Music educator and impresario.

Born into a musical family in Puerto Rico, Casals Istomin received a scholarship to study cello at the Mannes College of Music in Manhattan. She met Pablo Casals at the Prades Music Festival in France when she was 15. Impressed with her playing, he invited her to be his student. They were married in 1957, when she was 21 years old and he was 81. Together they pursued many musical projects, organizing festivals and travelling concerts, and founding the Puerto Rico Symphony and the Puerto Rico Conservatory of Music. After Pablo's death in 1973, Marta Casals began teaching cello at the Curtis Institute of Music in Philadelphia while continuing to run music festivals in Europe. She met the pianist Eugene Istomin and married him in 1975. In 1992 Casals Istomin was named president of the Manhattan School of Music, a post she held until 2005. She retains a seat on the board of directors.

Pablo Casals (1876–1973)

Spanish-born cellist, conductor, and composer.

Casals was best known as a cellist, making his Carnegie Hall debut in 1904. Throughout his long career, Casals pioneered many innovations in cello technique that made the instrument easier to play. Following the rise of fascist dictator Francisco Franco in Spain, Casals lived in exile, first in Prades in Catalonia, and finally settling in Puerto Rico, his mother's native land. With his wife, he cofounded the Puerto Rico Symphony Orchestra in 1958 and the Conservatory of Music of Puerto Rico in 1959. He was awarded the Medal of Freedom by President Kennedy in 1963. At the age of 80, Casals married a woman sixty years his junior, Marta Montáñez y Martínez. He dismissed concerns about the age difference with the retort: "I look at it this way: If she dies, she dies."

William Chapman (1923–2012)

Baritone.

Chapman started out as an actor, landing minor parts in Hollywood films before pursuing vocal training and ending up in New York in 1954. He acted in numerous musicals and first appeared on Broadway in Leonard Bernstein's *Candide* in 1956. As an opera singer he made his debut with the NBC Opera Theater in 1957. He went on to have an extensive career as a leading singer with the New York City Opera from 1957 to 1979. He was also a guest artist in opera productions worldwide. He retired to southern California where he taught voice on the faculty of the University of San Diego.

Janelle Corman (No information available)
Janey Corman (No information available)

George Coulouris (1903–1989)
English-born actor of stage and screen.
Coulouris made his London stage debut in 1926 but soon emigrated to New York. There he met Orson Welles, and the two became friends and collaborators on many theater projects throughout the 1930s, on radio as well as the stage. Coulouris played Walter Parks Thatcher in Welles's *Citizen Kane* (1941), a role for which he won a National Board of Review award. Coulouris returned to England in 1950, acting in over 80 films and appearing frequently on television. Coulouris was known for playing villains or other unsavory characters.

Albert Dekker (1905–1968)
American actor.
Born in New York City, Dekker gave up the study of medicine to become an actor. His Broadway debut came in Eugene O'Neill's *Marco Millions* in 1927. He moved to Hollywood 10 years later and starred in 70 films between the 1930s and 1960s. He was best known for playing a mad scientist in *Dr. Cyclops* and a criminal mastermind in *The Killers* in 1955. Dekkers dabbled in politics and was elected to the California gen-

eral assembly in the 1940s. He became an outspoken critic of Senator Joseph McCarthy's anticommunist crusade in the 1950s. Blacklisted in Hollywood, Dekker went back to work on Broadway.

William Dembaugh (1929-)

Longtime leading tenor of the New York City Opera, Dembaugh also had an extensive career as a guest soloist nationwide.

Pablo Elvira (1937–2000)

Baritone.
Born in Puerto Rico, Elvira began his musical career as a jazz trumpeter in his father's dance band. He was encouraged to switch to voice by the cellist Pablo Casals, who was then living in Puerto Rico. In 1960 Casals chose Elvira to perform the baritone part in his travelling production of his work *El Pessebre*. Later Elvira taught voice at the Indiana University School of Music. He moved to New York City in 1974 and commenced a singing career that featured many performances with both the Metropolitan and the New York City Operas. He also sang opera roles widely in Europe. In 1990 he retired to his home in Bozeman, Montana.

Richard Fredricks (1933-)

Baritone.
Born in Los Angeles, Fredricks was the leading dramatic baritone of both the New York City Opera and the Metropolitan Opera, debuting in 1960 and 1976, respectively. He has toured

in most major opera houses in the Americas, with some stints in Europe, particularly Germany, Italy, and the Netherlands. Fredricks made a few guest appearances playing himself in *The Odd Couple,* a primetime television sitcom that aired on ABC from 1970 to 1975. He has made numerous operatic and operetta recordings, most notably as Top in *The Tender Land* (with Norman Treigle, conducted by the composer, Aaron Copland) in 1965. Fredricks has also stage directed opera: *La Bohème* with both the Michigan Opera and the Duluth Opera, and *Manon* with the Honolulu Opera, in which he also sang the part of Lescaut. Fredricks resides in Los Angeles where he offers vocal coaching and singing lessons.

Livingston Gearhart (1916–1996)

Pianist, composer, arranger, and pedagogue.
Gearhart studied music at the Curtis Institute in Philadelphia and in France with Nadia Boulanger. From 1941 to 1954, Gearhart performed as part of a piano duo with Virginia Morley, clocking over 2,000 concerts throughout the United States and Canada and recording for major labels. Much of the duo's repertory was composed or arranged by Gearhart. They appeared frequently on the *Fred Waring Show*, a musical variety show that began on the radio and then was televised on CBS from 1949 to 1954. Gearhart was the show's arranger on staff. He is probably best known for a hit arrangement of the classic song "Dry Bones." Gearhart taught on the University of Buffalo Music Faculty from 1955 to 1985. He wrote or arranged many pieces for student singers and instrumentalists and authored a widely used series of teaching materials known as the *Sessions Series*.

Giuseppe Gismondo (1930–1998)

Italian tenor.

Gismondo was born in Sicily and studied music in Rome. As the 1950s began, he was making a career by singing in small and medium-sized theaters in Italy, but toward the end of the decade he branched out as a guest performer in international venues. His American debut was playing Pinkerton in *Madame Butterfly* at the New York City Opera in 1958. In 1959 he starred at the San Francisco Opera as Rodolfo in *La Bohème*. Gismondo's American appearances gave him the success he needed to break into the more illustrious opera houses of Europe, and although he maintained a lively schedule of guest appearances throughout the world, most of his remaining career was spent in Europe.

Igor Gorin (1904–1982)

Baritone.

Born Ignaz Greenberg in present-day Ukraine, Gorin's early life was focused on Jewish studies (his father was a rabbi). When he was 15, the family moved to Vienna, where Igor labored hard at various manual trades. A luckily timed audition for a local synagogue choir drew him the attention of Viktor Fuchs, an acclaimed vocal instructor. Through Fuchs, Gorin was able to study at the Vienna Music Academy from 1926 to 1929. He then became the lead cantor in a large Vienna synagogue and was quite famous. In 1930 he ended up at the Vienna Volksoper. However, the rise of nazism induced Gorin to emigrate to the United States in 1933. He sang at Radio City Music Hall and appeared frequently on radio and television during the 1930s and 1940s, singing selections from operas for various different broadcasters. This led to a career as a travelling opera singer in many regional companies, but he did not belong to any of them. Gorin married Mary Smith in 1939. Presumably, she is the wife Herb encountered.

Roy Harris (1898–1979)

American composer.

Born in Oklahoma, Harris grew up in rural southern California, the son of a farmer. When his father died, Roy sold the farm and supported himself by delivering milk. He enrolled in music at Berkeley, but was basically self-taught. A recommendation from Aaron Copland allowed him to study composition with Nadia Boulanger in Paris from 1926 to 1929. Back in the United States, he forged contacts with Howard Hanson, the director of the Eastman School of Music in Rochester, New York, where he continued his studies. In 1934, Harris's *Symphony No. 3* became the first American symphony to be commercially recorded, winning Harris broad fame. As a result, he was hired to teach at the Julliard School. However, a restless spirit kept him moving from place to place, teaching for short stints. Harris's music is known for the use of folk and jazz elements. His compositions number over 170 and include works for diverse ensembles of instruments, band, orchestra, voice, and chorus.

Bliss Hebert (1930–)

Opera stage director.

Born in Faust, New York, Hebert earned a master's degree in piano performance from Syracuse University. However, he quickly turned his talents toward opera, helping Igor Stravinsky stage and direct several of the composer's works, including five productions of *The Rake's Progress*. In the ensuing years, Hebert has directed or staged over 320 productions of 120 operas all over the world, with more than 70 premieres in partnership with his husband, Allen Charles Klein, as production designer. Hebert was the general manager of the Washington (DC) Opera Company from 1960 to 1964, and a founding member of the Santa Fe Opera Company, with which he was associated until 1986.

Marilyn Horne (1934 –)
Mezzo-soprano.

Horne was born in Pennsylvania, but moved to southern California as a child. She grew up in Hollywood and began singing backup for television jingles and covers for popular songs while in her teens. When Horne was 17, the famous German chanteuse Lotte Lehmann, then teaching at the Music Academy of the West in Santa Barbara, took her on as a protégé. Horne's first notable vocal employment came at the age of 20 when she dubbed the voice of the lead in the film *Carmen Jones* (1954), a movie adaptation of Bizet's opera *Carmen* featuring African American characters in a World War II setting. Igor Stravinsky took notice of her talents and brought her to Germany to sing in a music festival in Venice. She chose to remain in Europe, spending three seasons singing in the Gelsenkirchen Opera, and from there her opera engagements expanded internationally. Horne became part of a duo with Australian soprano Joan Sutherland, and the two toured extensively singing selections from the bel canto repertory. Although in demand from opera companies worldwide, it was only in 1970 that Horne finally made her Metropolitan debut in New York, playing the lead in Bellini's *Norma*. She then became a regular at that company into the 1980s. Horne was a special champion of American music, both contemporary compositions of the "classical" genre, and popular and traditional favorites. She also recorded many selections from musical theater and appeared on television in vaudeville-styled farcical operas with the comedian Carol Burnett. Horne retired from the concert stage in 1999. She was the director of the Music Academy of the West from 1997 to 2018 and currently resides in Santa Barbara.

Helen Hosmer (1898–1989)

Music educator.

Hosmer was born in Yonkers, New York, and grew up in Potsdam. A musical prodigy, by the age of 10 she was serving as an accompanist for teachers at the Crane School of Music, a division of the State University of New York. She also accompanied singers at the Potsdam Opera. After studying music for the summer of 1925 at the American Conservatory in Fontainebleau, France, Hosmer returned to the United States and earned her baccalaureate degree at the Teachers College of Columbia University. Hosmer was appointed the director of the Crane School in 1930 and served in that capacity until 1966. In retirement she travelled widely and was active in promoting many new methods, schools, and programs for music pedagogy and performance. In 1973 the Helen M. Hosmer Concert Hall at the Potsdam Campus was opened in her honor.

Danny Kaye (1911–1987)

American actor, comedian, dancer, and musician.

Born David Daniel Kaminsky in the Bronx, New York, Kaye began entertaining his classmates in school at an early age, but never graduated from high school. Instead, he led a nomadic life for a few years, taking a series of odd jobs from which he was almost always fired. He landed in the famous Catskills resorts of the Borscht Belt, where many Jewish comedians got their start. Kaye began by introducing acts and performing stand-up comedy routines. He featured a lot of physical humor, especially pantomime, and tongue-twisting patter songs. Kaye started hosting his own radio show in 1945 and first appeared on television in 1956. He had his own television variety show, *The Danny Kaye Show*, from 1963 to 1967, and starred in 17 movies over the span of his career. Kaye also appeared as a guest on innumerable other shows and performed internationally, being a special favorite of the British royal family. Much of Kaye's comic material, including his songs, were written by his wife, Sylvia Fine. Danny Kaye was also a noted philanthropist, baseball enthusiast, amateur chef, and pilot.

Ruth Kobart (1924–2002)

A versatile singer of both opera and musical theater works. Kobart was born in Des Moines, Iowa, and studied music at the American Conservatory in Chicago. She made her Broadway debut in 1953 in the chorus of Rogers and Hammerstein's musical *Pipe Dream*. She was a frequent performer with the NBC Opera Theatre and the New York City Opera. Kobart was also an actress in nonmusical works. She specialized in character roles and is perhaps best known for her portrayal of Nurse Ratched in *One Flew Over the Cuckoo's Nest* by Ken Kesey. Kobart had a long association with the San Francisco American Conservatory Theater that began in 1967 and lasted until 1994. She also played many roles in films and on television, frequently portraying villainesses.

Josef Krips (1902–1974)

Austrian-born conductor and violinist.
Krips was conductor of the Wiener Stadsoper and a professor at the Vienna Academy of Fine Arts when he was forced to flee Austria by the Nazis in 1938. He waited out the duration of the war in Yugoslavia, where he worked in a food factory. Although Krips was later welcomed back to Austria, he eventually chose the life of an expatriate, becoming the principal conductor of the London Symphony Orchestra from 1950 to 1954. He then came to the United States where he led the Buffalo Philharmonic Orchestra until 1963, when he took over conducting the San Francisco Symphony until 1970. Krips also maintained an active schedule as a guest conductor worldwide. Initially, Krips was known for rigidly classical programming, much of which is preserved in commercial recordings. However, during his years in San Francisco, he warmed up to contemporary twentieth-century music, even programming several world premieres of modern American works. In 1970, Krips returned to Europe, taking over the Deutsche Oper in Berlin and becoming the principal conductor of the Vienna Symphony Orchestra until 1973.

Normand Lockwood (1906–2002)

American composer.
Born in New York City, Lockwood studied music at the University of Michigan. He made his way to Rome in the mid-

1920s and studied composition under Ottorino Respighi and Nadia Boulanger. Lockwood is best known for choral works based on religious texts. But he also wrote five operas, a symphony, a concerto for organ, and numerous chamber works for various ensembles of instruments, as well as choral works. Lockwood taught at Oberlin Conservatory in Oberlin, Ohio; Colombia University in New York; Trinity College in Texas; the universities of Wyoming, Oregon, and Hawaii, and ended up at the University of Denver, where he was composer-in-residence from 1961 to 1974.

Chester "Chet" Ludgin (1925–2003)

Operatic baritone.

A native of Brooklyn, New York, Ludgin had his operatic debut with the New York City Opera in 1957 and appeared with that company in more than 30 roles over the years. His greatest role was probably playing John Proctor in the world premiere of *The Crucible* by Robert Ward in 1961. Ludgin also had a long association with the San Francisco Opera from 1962 to 1985. With a voice the critics described as "noble" and "rich," Ludgin was also especially praised for his acting ability.

Ludwig Lustig (1900–1994)

Lustig was a manager and agent for opera singers and other classical musicians from 1941 into the 1970s. At one time he had as many as 250 New York City Opera members as his clients. His most famous client may have been the soprano Beverly Sills, whom he represented for 23 years.

Michele Molese (1928–1989)

Tenor.

Born in New York City as Michael Kenneth Pratt, Molese studied music in Italy. His debut in Milan came in 1956, when he played Beppo in *Pagliacci*. He sang in the Dutch opera, concertized, and spend a few seasons as the leading tenor in the Belgrade (Yugoslavia) Opera. In 1964, he returned to the United States and joined the New York City Opera, appearing first as Pinkerton in *Madame Butterfly*. His voice has been described as "sturdy" and he often played leading man to Beverly Sills. After hitting a high C in a 1974 performance of *Un ballo in maschera*, Molese addressed the powerful *New York Times* music critic directly from the stage, saying "That pinched high C is for Mr. Schonberg." Julius Rudel, the director of the NYCO, fired him for unprofessional conduct. But despite Rudel's wish, Molese was hired back and appeared in almost every major tenor role, giving his final performance for the NYCO six years later.

Robert Merrill (1917–2004)

Baritone and actor.

Merrill was the son of Jewish immigrants from Poland. His mother arranged for him to have early voice lessons, partly to remedy a stutter that disappeared when he sang, and Merrill conceived a love of opera. He later paid for his voice lessons by working semi-professionally as a baseball pitcher. However, Merrill got his real start as a crooner in the Borscht Belt resort circuit in upper-New York state. An agent he met there got him work at Radio

City Music Hall and the NBC Symphony Orchestra under Arturo Toscanini. He won the Metropolitan Opera Auditions of the Air contest in 1945 and made his Metropolitan Opera debut the same year. By 1960 he was the Met's leading baritone, a position he occupied until 1976. Merrill is featured in many of the era's outstanding opera recordings. He also appeared extensively on radio and television and sang many recitals all over the country. Merrill's lifelong love of baseball led him to be the featured singer of *The Star Spangled Banner* for many years at Yankee Stadium to open every baseball season.

Zero Mostel (1915–1977)

American actor, comedian, and singer.
Born in Brooklyn, New York, Samuel Mostel was the class clown from an early age and wanted to be a painter. The young Mostel copied paintings at the Metropolitan Museum of Art and entertained onlookers with comic antics at the same time. He graduated from the City College of New York in 1935, and the Works Progress Administration's Federal Art Project hired him to teach art and lead tours of art museums. Mostel's tours were so entertaining that he developed a reputation. This led to paid appearances at private parties and eventually to being hired as a professional comedian by a Manhattan nightclub. A press agent dubbed him "Zero" because he was "starting from nothing." Mostel's comic career took off and soon he was acting on Broadway and appearing on the radio. During WWII, an injury prevented him from active duty, so he toured with the USO entertaining the troops. Long attracted to liberal causes, Mostel was called before the nefarious

House Un-American Activities Committee to testify during the red scare years of the 1950s. He cracked jokes, refused to name names, and generally demeaned the proceedings. Though praised for his bravery, Mostel was blacklisted and his career took a dive. It began to revive when he won rave reviews for his roles as Pseudolus in the Broadway musical *A Funny Thing Happened on the Way to the Forum* in 1962 and Tevje in *Fiddler on the Roof* in 1964. Although Mostel appeared in films and on television for the rest of his life, his brand of humor went into decline. He died of an aortic aneurism when he was 62.

Maralin Niska (1926–2016)

American operatic soprano and singing actor.

Niska was born in San Pedro, California. She studied at UCLA and worked as a public school teacher for seven years after graduating with a degree in English. Niska went back to UCLA to study voice in the 1950s and got her start singing roles for regional opera companies in southern California. In 1965, she was cast in the title role in Carlisle Floyd's *Susannah* in a production put on by the Metropolitan Opera National Company in Indianapolis. Her performance there brought her to national notice, and two years later she made her New York debut with the New York City Opera as Countess Almaviva in *Le nozze di Figaro* opposite Norman Treigle. This began her association with that company that ultimately saw her perform 29 leading roles, a record at the time. Niska also appeared with the Metropolitan Opera and had an extensive career as a guest star in companies throughout the United States and internationally. She retired to Santa Fe, New Mexico.

Robert O'Hearn (1921–2016)

American set designer.

O'Hearn was born in Elkhart, Indiana, and graduated with a BA from Indiana University in 1943. He made his debut as a set designer on Broadway in 1950. Within three years he was working regularly designing sets for Broadway companies, including the Metropolitan Opera. In all he designed 13 productions for the Met, including the set and costumes for Donizetti's *L'elisir d'amore*. It was in this production that O'Hearn had the character of Dr. Dulcamara make his entrance by hot air balloon—an innovation that became a convention for companies that could afford it. O'Hearn went on to become a sought-after designer for other opera companies, including the New York City Opera and companies in Chicago, Houston, and Los Angeles, as well as for Canadian and European productions as well. O'Hearn was a professor at the New York Studio and Forum of Stage Design from 1968 to 1988. He then taught at the Jacobs School of Music at Indiana University, from which he retired in 2008.

Eugene Ormandy (1899–1985)

Orchestra conductor.

Born in Hungary as Jeno Blau, by the age of five he was the youngest student ever admitted to the Royal Academy of Music in Budapest. By 10 he was playing violin for the Austro-Hungarian royalty. Graduated at 14, by 17 he was already a professor and touring Europe as a concert soloist. In 1921, Ormandy was lured to the United States by the prospect of an American tour. Legend has it that he decided to change his name on the voyage over the

Atlantic, choosing "Ormandy" in honor of the ship he was on, the *S.S. Normandie*. In any case, the promised tour fell through and Ormandy was stranded in New York, nearly penniless. He was hired to play in the orchestra of the Capitol Theatre, which accompanied silent films, and was promoted immediately to concertmaster. He then began to fill in for the conductor and free-lancing other conducting jobs. The powerful agent Arthur Judson helped Ormandy land a conducting gig at the Philadelphia Symphony Orchestra when Arturo Toscanini fell ill in 1931. His success there led to a position as conductor of the Minneapolis Symphony. In 1938, Ormandy took over from Leopold Stokowski as music director and conductor of the Philadelphia Symphony Orchestra. He was to remain in this position for the next 44 years, developing what became known as the "Philadelphia sound" – lush, opulent, and smooth. Some, notably Leonard Bernstein, criticized Ormandy for never varying the orchestra's sound, even when it was out of character for the piece at hand. Nevertheless, such was the group's popularity that Ormandy toured with it all over the world and made so many recordings of all genres, from acoustical to digital formats, that it was said that the Philadelphia Orchestra had recorded the "complete works of everybody"— sometimes more than once.

David Poleri (1927–1967)

American tenor.

Born in Philadelphia, Pennsylvania, Poleri made his opera debut in Chicago in *Faust* in 1950. After that he was employed as a guest artist in many productions throughout the country, although he never made it to the Metropolitan Opera. He had a steady job singing for the NBC Television Opera Theater beginning in 1950. Poleri is famous for committing "career suicide" during one performance of *Carmen* in Chicago in 1953 put on by the New York City Opera. Poleri was playing the role of Carmen's jealous lover, Don Jose. Exasperated by the fast tempos that the conductor, Joseph Rosenstock, was taking in the final scene, Poleri threw down the knife with which he was to kill Carmen, yelled "Finish it yourself!" to Rosenstock, and stormed off the stage. The soprano playing Carmen, Gloria Lane, had to pretend to simply drop dead and an understudy for Poleri finished the part from the wings. This incident pretty much ended Poleri's career in America. He had some later success singing in Europe. Poleri was killed in a helicopter crash while visiting Hawaii at the age of 40.

Frank Porretta (1930–2015)

American tenor.

Porretta was born in Detroit, Michigan, and graduated from the University of Michigan with a bachelor's degree in music in 1952. He joined the army that same year and began his singing career with the U.S. Army Band choir. In 1954 he won a scholarship to study voice in New York City. His professional debut with the New York City Opera came in 1956 as Frederic in *Mignon*, with Beverly Sills as Philine. He remained with the NYCO until 1970, but toured as a guest artist with many other companies. Porretta also performed in light operas such as those by Gilbert and Sullivan and Bertolt Brecht, and in many American musicals. Still in his early forties, he retired from the stage and spent the next forty years as a church choir director in Darien, Connecticut.

Frederick Ressel (1899–1999)

Ressel was principal violist with the Buffalo Philharmonic Orchestra for 41 years, having helped found the group in 1935. He was also a teacher of music and viola privately and in high schools in the Buffalo area.

Joaquin Romaguera (1932–)

American operatic tenor and musical theater actor and singer. Born in Key West, Florida, Romaguera received early training with the Florida Opera Guild. He performed at Radio City Music Hall and then joined the New York City Opera in 1965. Romaguera also directed operas, such as *Aida* in the Colorado Opera Festival in 1977. His fame, however, rests mostly on his work in musical theater, where he specialized in playing humorous character roles, often in operatic style. Most notably Romaguera originated the role of the flamboyant barber Adolfo Pirelli in Sondheim's *Sweeney Todd* in 1979. He also created roles in the original productions of *Fiorello* (1997) and *Evita* (2000).

Joseph Rosenstock (1895–1985)

Orchestral and opera conductor.
Rosenstock was born in Krakow, Poland, and studied at the Academy of Music in Vienna. By the age of 21 he was conducting the Vienna Philharmonic Choir. In 1929 he came to New

York to conduct German operas for the Metropolitan Opera Company. He lasted only three weeks on the job, as a storm of negative reviews convinced him to quit and go back to Germany. In 1936, Rosenstock left Germany for Japan, where he conducted the Japan Symphony Orchestra. In 1948 he returned to New York as a conductor for the New York City Opera. This time reviews were positive and he remained. In 1952 he became general director of the company. Rosenstock was known for innovative programming and he was the first to include musical theater in the NYCO's season. It was a decision for which he took much criticism. However, the shows played to packed houses. In 1955 Rosenstock returned to Japan for several years. He was hired by the Metropolitan Opera again in 1961. There he remained until 1969, having conducted 248 opera performances for the company.

Julius Rudel (1921–2014)

Opera conductor.

Rudel and his family arrived in New York from Vienna in 1938, among the many Jews fleeing Hitler. He joined the New York City Opera in 1944, shortly after it was formed, and went on to become both its principal conductor and director from 1957 to 1979. Rudel is credited with raising that organization to world-class heights while still keeping ticket prices low and taking chances on producing contemporary American musicals and operas, as well as the old European operatic war horses. He nurtured new talent, giving such stars as Beverly Sills, José Carreras, and Sherrill Milnes their starts. Rudel was also a frequent guest conductor throughout the United States and abroad. He conducted over 200 performances at the Metropolitan Opera and he served as music director for the Kennedy Center for the Performing Arts from 1971 to 1975.

Kurt Saffir (1929–1988)

Opera conductor, accompanist, and vocal coach.
Born in Vienna, Saffir came to the United States in 1938. He studied piano and conducting at the Julliard School, graduating with a master's degree in 1952. He was an assistant conductor and vocal coach at the New York City Opera from 1953 to 1963. Saffir then conducted the Dortmund Opera in West Germany until 1967. Back in the United States, Saffir was instrumental in organizing and conducting many opera festivals on the East Coast. He also mounted several opera productions with the Central City Opera in Colorado. Residing in New York City, he continued to be sought after as a vocal coach and accompanist throughout his career.

Alexander Schneider (1908–1993)

Violinist, conductor, and educator.
Schneider was born in Vilnius, Lithuania. A child prodigy, by the age of 10 he was studying violin at the music conservatory there. He moved to Germany and became the concertmaster of the Frankfurt Museum Orchestra while still in his teens. In 1932 he joined the renowned Budapest String Quartet as second violinist. His brother was already the group's cellist. In 1939 the quartet was on tour in the United States when war broke out in Europe. The

members were granted asylum and made the new country their home. Schneider left the quartet in 1944. For the next ten years he took gigs playing with several other chamber ensembles. During this time he coaxed the cellist Pablo Casals back into musical relevancy by helping found the Casals Festival in Prades, Spain, where Casals was then living in self-imposed exile. Schneider became Casals's righthand man in many musical endeavors, including organizing other music festivals all over the world. Schneider formed his own string quartet in 1952. In addition to his concertizing, Schneider maintained an active career as a guest conductor and teacher. He championed or mentored young artists and ensembles, many of whom went on to illustrious careers. In 1972, Schneider formed his own chamber orchestra, the Brandenburg Ensemble. With this group and others Schneider made hundreds of recordings, notably championing the music of Haydn and Bach.

Harold Schonberg (1915–2003)

American journalist and critic.

Born in New York City, Schonberg was very talented musically. But he was unusual in deciding while still a child that he wanted to write about music instead of performing it. He graduated from Brooklyn College in 1937 where he had already been writing reviews for the college paper. Schonberg joined the U.S. Army and served during World War II as a codebreaker in London. Back in the United States, he pursued his dream and by 1955 was the senior music critic of the *New York Times*. In 1971 Schonberg became the first person to receive a Pulitzer prize for music criticism. Schonberg also wrote books about music–13 in all–among which *The Great Pianists* and *Lives of the Great Composers* have become standard reference works. With a powerful musical memory (he could know a piece after a single hearing) and background knowledge based on tireless study, Schonberg naturally achieved influence in the musical world. A competent pianist himself, he was especially focused on evaluating pianists. His writing style was spare and lucid, but he could employ an unusual adjective or metaphor to advantage. Schonberg was also known for responding to readers' queries about all sorts of peripheral matters, such as whether house lights should be left on or whether it was seemly for listeners to follow a score during performances. He also reviewed musical recordings, reported on a number of international chess competitions, and under a pseudonym wrote reviews of murder mysteries and detective thrillers for 25 years.

Robert Shaw (1916–1999)

American choral conductor.

Shaw was born in Red Bluff, California, the son of a preacher. He attended Pomona College, majoring in religion and philosophy. As the leader of the college glee club, he came to the attention of Fred Waring, who hosted a popular radio show. Waring hired Shaw to lead the Fred Waring Glee Club in New York, in which position Shaw served from 1938 to 1945. In 1948 Shaw founded a professional group of 40 singers, the Robert Shaw Chorale. This group's success touring and recording led to Shaw's employment as conductor of the San Diego Symphony from 1953 to 1958 and associate conductor of the

Cleveland Orchestra under George Szell from 1956 to 1967. In 1967 Shaw moved to Atlanta where he founded and conducted the Atlanta Symphony Chamber Chorus and Atlanta Orchestra Chorus until 1988. In 1990 he was hired to lead workshops in vocal ensemble singing at Carnegie Hall in New York. Over the years, Shaw became one of the most influential choral conductors in the world. He pioneered special rehearsal techniques that isolated features of pitch, rhythm, and enunciation in choral works. He made sure singers understood the spiritual or philosophical meaning of vocal texts, as this would influence the mood or feeling of a piece. Shaw was known for mentoring talented young singers, for promoting contemporary choral music, and for generally raising the standards of choral conducting. Many recordings of Shaw-led groups won awards and are regarded as benchmarks of choral excellence today.

Beverly Sills (1929–2007)

American soprano.

Sills was born Belle Silverman in Brooklyn, New York, to Jewish immigrants. She was singing and performing by the age of three, and was cast in children's films and performed on radio shows from the age of four. She began taking voice lessons at nine. Sills was a graduate of Erasmus Hall High School in Brooklyn and the Manhattan Professional Children's School. In 1945, she made her adult debut performing in the light opera of Gilbert and Sullivan, developing a superb sense of comic timing that she used to advantage for the rest of her life. In 1947, Sills made her serious opera debut with the Philadelphia Civic Grand Opera Company as the gypsy Frasquita in Bizet's *Carmen*. Soon she was in demand at opera companies all over the country. From 1960 throughout the 1970s, her reputation grew. In 1971 Sills appeared on the cover of *Time* magazine, described as "America's Queen of Opera." Sills is credited with popularizing opera for American audiences, appearing on radio and television talk shows to present an appealing "human" face to an art form that was still considered stuffy and European. Sills's voice has been described as "silvery," "supple," and "enveloping." She was known for effortlessly spinning out notes above high C with a diamond clarity that cut through the thickest orchestrations. In her later years, Sills took on management roles at several performing arts organizations, starting in 1979 with the New York City Opera for ten years and as chairwoman of Lincoln Center from 1994 to 2002. From 2002 to 2005 she was chairwoman of the Metropolitan Opera Company. Sills was also known as a philanthropist, particularly for causes associated with the prevention of birth defects.

William Steinberg (1899–1978)

German-born conductor.

Musically talented, Steinberg was conducting his own compositions by the age of 13. He graduated from the Cologne Conservatory of Music and at the age of 23 became assistant conductor to Otto Klemperer at the Cologne Opera. In 1924, he took over as principal conductor. But in 1933 he was fired from his then-post conducting the Frankfurt Opera because he was Jewish. Seeing the drift of European politics, Steinberg left Europe for Palestine, where he was conducting the Palestine Symphony Orchestra when Arturo Toscanini visited in 1936. Impressed by what he saw, Toscanini hired Steinberg two years later to help prepare the NBC Symphony Orchestra broadcasts in New York. Steinberg took conducting posts at several orchestras (New York Philharmonic, Buffalo, San Francisco Opera) before settling with the Pittsburgh Symphony Orchestra from 1952 to 1976. He maintained an active career as a guest conductor worldwide at the same time, once observing that conducting was the profession of "travelling salesmen." Steinberg and the Pittsburgh Symphony were in demand by major recording companies and left a legacy of some of the finest recordings of major classical works. Steinberg also premiered numerous contemporary works and championed some lesser-known older works. Steinberg was known for a sense of humor and not taking himself too seriously, at the same time he was roundly praised for his musical sophistication and understated, calm conducting style.

John Charles Thomas (1891–1960)

American baritone.

Born in Meyersdale, Pennsylvania, Thomas received a scholarship in 1910 to study voice at the Peabody Institute in Baltimore, Maryland. He moved to New York and got his start singing the light operas of Gilbert and Sullivan. The age of the American musical was dawning and Thomas was in on the start. For the next decade he was a Broadway musical theater star. In 1925 he played his first serious opera role in Verdi's *Aida* with the

Washington National Opera. A stint playing in the opera halls of Europe solidified his operatic reputation. He returned to the United States and made pioneering recordings and appeared frequently on the radio. He became a staple at the Metropolitan Opera in New York from 1934 to 1943, but continued to play opera houses all over the country. Thomas was the rare performer who was equally at home in the classical or popular repertory and could play either serious or comedic roles with equal skill. In his day, he was one of the most sought after singers in the country.

Robert Trehy (1921–2009)

American baritone.
Trehy was born in New York City, served in the armed forces in World War II, and only after the war studied music at the Mannes School of Music in Manhattan, majoring in voice. He continued his vocal studies in Vienna and began appearing on European opera stages in the 1950s. As that decade came to a close, Trehy moved back to the United States, where he appeared with opera companies all over the country into the 1980s. In 1969 Trehy joined the voice faculty at Pennsylvania State University where he taught for 14 years.

Norman Treigle (1927–1975)

American operatic bass-baritone.
Treigle was born in New Orleans to a poor family. He did not begin voice studies until 1946 and made his opera debut the following year with the New Orleans Opera Association. He studied music

at Loyola University in New Orleans from 1949 to 1951, while continuing to perform with local groups. In 1953 Treigle made his debut at the New York City Opera in *La Bohème*. Three years later he achieved his first significant notice in the opera world by his portrayal of Reverend Olin Blitch in Carlisle Floyd's opera *Susannah*. His European debut came in the same role at the Brussels World's Fair in 1958. Rail thin with craggy features and perpetual deep circles under his eyes, Treigle presented a dream countenance for character roles. At the same time, his extraordinary acting ability put him foremost among the world's so-called singing actors. His personal magnetism was such that audiences focused on him even when he was not singing. Yet it was his voice and musicality that won over critics. One review described his voice as "having a color of crude oil—dark, flexible." Not surprisingly Treigle specialized in sinister roles, his most famous being Mephistofele in both *Faust* by Gounod and *Mephistofele* by Boito. However, he was versatile and covered the repertory from Handel to Puccini and Mozart to Offenbach. Personally, Treigle was beset by demons, and his offstage life was erratic, complicated, and sordid, including gambling and adultery. He was a chain smoker and heavy drinker. He suffered inordinately from insomnia. In 1975, at the age of 47, he was found dead in his apartment of an apparent overdose of barbiturate sleeping pills. Treigle's biographer, Brian Morgan, described him as a "comet streaking across the operatic sky."

Tatiana Troyanos (1938–1993)

Mezzo-soprano.

Troyanos was born in New York City to a Greek father and German mother who were both aspiring opera singers. They divorced when Troyanos was still an infant, and she was mostly raised in an orphanage. It was here that she began singing lessons, offered by local musicians as charity to the children there. Troyanos continued her music studies on scholarship at the Brooklyn Music School. A teacher helped her get into the Julliard School. Troyanos began to garner notice in the various ensembles she sang with, ranging from church choirs to musical theater groups, even as she took employment as a secretary for a publishing house. After a long run in the chorus of *The Sound of Music,* she was cast by the New York City Opera in 1963 in *A Mid Summer's Night's Dream.* In spite of increasing offers of roles in both the NYCO and the Metropolitan, Troyanos chose to move to Germany in 1965, in search of advanced training and performing opportunities. She stayed there for a decade building a significant career. Troyanos's voice has been described as "sumptuous" and many noted the sense of determination behind it, which Troyanos herself attributed to her lifelong insecurities. Troyanos returned to New York and became a staple with the Metropolitan Opera from 1976 to her death in 1993 from breast cancer. She left behind an extensive record of her vocal accomplishments in recorded performances.

Lee Venora (1932–)
American operatic and musical theater soprano.
Born in Bridgeport, Connecticut, Venora studied music at the Hartt School in the University of Hartford. In 1958 she made her debut with the New York City Opera and went on to play many roles for that company. In 1959 she began an association with Leonard Ber-

nstein, singing in many roles for the New York Philharmonic where Bernstein was conducting. This led to television appearances with the group as well. Venora also sang in light opera such as Gilbert and Sullivan and musical theater and seemed equally at home there as on the operatic stage. She was well known for leading roles in the revivals of the musicals *Carousel* and *Kismet*. Venora appeared frequently with the San Francisco Opera from 1961 to 1964. She was in demand as a guest star for many companies throughout the United States as well as maintaining an active schedule as a recitalist.

Arnold Voketaitis (1930 –)
American bass-baritone.
Voketaitis was born in New Haven, Connecticut, and graduated from Quinnipiac University. He studied voice with several teachers, including Kurt Saffir, in New York City, before he joined the U.S. Army in the 1950s. There he began singing with the Army Band in 1956. Winning several vocal competitions earned him an opera debut with the New York City Opera in the 1958 performance of *The Silent Woman* by Richard Strauss. Other roles followed, and Voketaitis became a regular with the NYCO until 1981. He was a popular guest artist with opera companies throughout the United States for 30 years beginning in the 1960s. Leonard Bernstein praised him as a "musical asset." Voketaitis was also engaged on the singing faculties of a number of American colleges, including Auburn University in Alabama, De Paul University in Chicago, and Northwestern University in Illinois.

Margaret Webster (1905–1972)

American-British actress, theater and opera director, and author. Webster spent her childhood in both New York and London while her parents, both prominent English actors, toured the world. Webster's mother began reading Shakespeare to her when she was three years old, and she was often allowed to watch her parents performing from the wings and even to join in crowd scenes on the stage. Webster made her own stage debut at the age of eight in a play directed by the famous actress Ellen Terry. Webster graduated from the Etlinger Dramatic School in London in 1923. She spent the next decade honing her skills as an actress and director in companies playing throughout the United Kingdom. By 1936, she had come to the attention of Maurice Evans, a noted director, who invited her to direct his New York production of *Richard II*. The first Broadway presentation of the play since 1878, it was a tremendous success and led to more directing opportunities, even as Webster continued her acting career. In 1942 Webster took the daring step of casting African American actor Paul Robeson as Othello. In spite of dire warnings that this would keep patrons away, the production beat box office records. Webster thereafter made unusual casting part of her directing style. In the 1940s Webster founded her own theater companies and toured with them within the United States and Canada. The mostly Shakespeare productions solidified her reputation. In 1950, Webster became the first woman to direct an opera at the Metropolitan Opera Company in New York. It was Verdi's *Don Carlos*. Her success there led to other opera conducting engagements, including Strauss's *The Silent Woman* in 1958 for the New York City Opera. Sometime in the 1950s Webster was denounced to the House Un-American Affairs Committee in Congress as a communist sympathizer. Blacklisted in the United States, she then returned to England where she continued to act and direct. In the 1960s, the red scare in the past, she was a frequent guest lecturer at American colleges and universities. Webster was the author of three books: *Shakespeare Without Tears*, *The Same Only Different* (about her family), and *Don't Put Your Daughter on the Stage* (an autobiography). She died in London of colon cancer at the age of 67.

John Simon White (1910–2001)

Opera voice coach, stage director, and administrator.

Born in Vienna as Hans Schwarzkopf, White earned a PhD from the University of Vienna in 1933. After study in France and Italy, he came to the United States in 1938, one among a wave of talented Jewish musicians fleeing the Nazis. In America he was reduced to hauling produce for a time, then taught German and aided French refugees. He became a U.S. citizen while serving in the U.S. Army during World War II. He was hired as a voice coach for the New York City Opera in 1946. Although White stage directed for the opera, his biggest contribution was behind the scenes in administrative work. He handled budgets and negotiations with performers, as well as joining in "scouting" expeditions to find and hire new talent. Along with Julius Rudel and Felix Popper, who were both conductors, White was part of a "troika" that managed the NYCO organization throughout the decades of the 1950s through 1970s. White was named associate director of the organization in 1952, and rose to managing director in 1968, a post he held until his retirement in 1980. He continued to be a consultant for the company until his death. White was a popular figure with the artists who performed at the NYCO. Soprano Beverly Sills described him as a gentleman of impeccable Old World manners and refined tastes.

John C. Wilcox (1870–1947)

Vocal instructor.
John C. "Daddy" Wilcox was a legendary voice teacher who taught at the American Conservatory of Music in Chicago, among other places. He was beloved of his students, among whom was Herbert Beattie. Wilcox spent several summers as an artist-in-residence at Colorado College in Colorado Springs, Colorado. While there he enticed the young Beattie to spend a summer session studying voice and it left a lasting impression, enough to draw Beattie back for college and later to live in this city on the front range. Wilcox wrote an influential book on vocal production entitled *The Living Voice: A Study Guide for Song and Speech* (1935). Wilcox spent the last two years of his life in Colorado Springs and continued to teach voice up until his death.

John Finley Williamson (1887–1964)

American choral conductor.
One of the most influential choral conductors of the twentieth century, Williamson was born in Canton, Ohio, to English immigrants. His talent for singing was apparent from childhood and he eventually developed into an excellent baritone. Williamson

majored in music at Otterbein College in Westerville, Ohio. After graduation he founded and directed the Westminster Choir at the Westminster Presbyterian Church in Dayton, Ohio. Realizing that the sound could be greatly improved by engaging professionally trained singers, Williamson founded the Westminster Choir School in 1926. It started with 60 students and a faculty of 10. The school was so successful that it was soon necessary to expand it. With Williamson at its helm, the school eventually moved to Princeton, New Jersey, where it changed its name to Westminster Choir College and continues to train singers to this day. Under Williamson's direction, the Westminster Choir became one of the best and most sought-after choral groups in the world. Eventually comprising more than 100 singers, the Choir toured and performed with nearly every major orchestra and under illustrious conductors. It made recordings with major record labels that are considered benchmarks of excellence. In 1934, the Choir was even heard in a rare broadcast from the Soviet Union. Williamson was famous for teaching students to conduct without using their hands. According to him, through a process of "melodic sculpting," the choral conductor must set the mood, breath, pace, and attack for the piece being performed. He urged singers to feel the amplitude, frequency, and overtones in notes and to find the "soul" of a piece. Following his retirement in 1958 from the Choir College, Williamson continued to give choral workshops to groups all over the world.

Acknowledgments

I would like to acknowledge my publisher Don Kallaus for all his advice and hard work in preparing my book and my wonderful friend and editor, Lauren Arnest, who has been an inspiration through the tough times getting this book ready. Also, I want to thank my beloved wife Laurie for all she has done to help me finish this endeavor.

Index

A

Abduction from the Seraglio, 35–36, 88
Academy of Music in Philadelphia, 18–20, 72
Adler, Kurt Herbert, 30–32, 93
Adler, Peter Herman, 13–16, 94
Alessandro, Victor, 38–39, 94
Arshansky, Michael, 85, 94
Auden, W. H., *x*

B

Barber of Seville, 29, 38–39, 77, 83–84
Basile, Arturo, 39–41, 95
Beattie, Herbert
   About the Author, 87–91
   in Colorado Springs, *ix–xii*, 87, 91
   comic roles, 2, 83–84
   photographs, 48–60
   student of John C. Wilcox, 131
Bernstein, Leonard, 41–42, 95–96, 100, 115, 127–128
Bohème, La, 29, 103–104, 126
Boulanger, Lili, 97
Boulanger, Nadia, 42–43, 97
Buckley, Emerson, 32–34, 97–98
Carole Bogard, 50, 66, 96

C
Caldwell, Sarah, 28–30, 69, 98
Callaway, Paul, 98
Carnegie Hall, 41, 100, 122
Carrnen, 29, 72, 106, 116, 123
Casals, Pablo, *xi*, 21–25, 49, 89, 99, 100–102, 120
Cavalleria Rusticana, 29
Chapman, William, 40–41, 100–101
Childhood of Christ, The, 19, 72
choral conducting, 25–26, 122
comic roles, 2, 83–84
conductors, 11–46
Copland, Aaron, 42–43
Corman sisters, 81–83, 101
Coulouris, George, 6, 101

D
Dekker, Albert, 35–36, 101–102
Dembaugh, William, 17, 102
Don Giovanni, 37, 54–55, 75, 77
Don Pasquale, 44–45, 55, 57, 71, 84

E
Elvira, Pablo, 24, 102

F
Faust, 29, 50, 71, 115, 126
Fledermaus, 29
Fredricks, Richard, 67, 102–103

G
Gearhart, Livingston, 81–83, 103
Gismondo, Giiuseppe, 40, 104
Gorin, Igor, 73–74, 104

H
Harris, Roy, 26, 105
Hebert, Bliss, 31, 105
Horne, Marilyn, 93, 106–107
    photographs, 59
Hosmer, Helen, 42–43, 107

I
Istomin, Marta Casals, 98
Italian Girl in Algiers, 37, 52, 58–60, 66, 84

K
Kaye, Danny, *xi*, 14, 107–108
Kobart, Ruth, 36–38, 108
Krips, Josef, 11–13, 34, 109

L
Lockwood, Normand, 27, 109
Ludgin, Chester, 36, 110
Lustig, Ludwig, 1, 14, 16, 83, 110

M
Macbeth, 39–40

Madame Butterfly, 2, 8, 29, 69, 85, 104, 111
Marriage of Figaro, The, 29, 113
Merrill, Robert, 73, 111
Messiah, 12, 19–21
Molese, Michele, 36–38, 71, 111
Mostel, Zero, *xii*, 17, 112–113

N
New York City Opera, 5, 13–16, 34, 36, 39, 84, 85, 88–89, 98–130
New York Metropolitan Opera, 114, 129
New York Philharmonic, 95, 124, 128
Niska, Maralin, 65, 113

O
O'Hearn, Robert, 112–113
opera companies, *xi*, 44–46, 88, 106, 113–114, 123, 125, 128
Opera Company of Boston, 28, 69, 98
opera life
   food, 6–7
   lodging, 4–6
   the payoff, 7–8
   shoes, 1–2, 71–72
   travel, 2–4
Ormandy, Eugene, 18–21, 72, 84, 89, 114–115

P
Pagliacci, 29, 111
photographs, 48–60

Pittsburgh Symphony, 16–18, 124
Poleri, David, 75, 115
Porretta, Frank, 72, 116

R
Ressell, Frederick, 117
Rigoletto, 29
Rise and Fall of the City of Mahoganny, The, 45, 64
Romaguerra, Joaquin, 117
Rosenstock, Joseph, 72, 116, 117
Rudel, Julius, 34–38, 77, 89, 111, 118, 130

S
Saffir, Kurt, 15, 119, 128
San Francisco Opera, *xi*, 30, 32, 93
Schneider, Alexander, 23–25, 119
Schonberg, Harold, 8, 120
Shaw, Robert, 1, 43, 120
Silent Woman, The, 13–16
Sills, Beverly, *xii*, 16–18, 38, 77, 110, 111, 116, 118, 122, 131
singers
    baritones, 73–74
    basses, 75–77
    gestures and habits, 63–65
    sopranos, 65–69
    tenors, 70–73
Steinberg, William, 16–18, 84, 89, 123
Stravinsky, Igor, 105, 106

T
Te Deum, The, 16–18
Thomas, John Charles, 77, 124
Toscanini, Arturo, 115, 124
Traviata, 29, 68
Trehy, Robert, 30, 125
Treigle, Norman, 5, 13, 38, 77, 103, 113, 125–126
Troyanos, Tatiana, 30, 126–127

V
Venora, Lee, 67–68, 127
Voketaitis, Arnold, 38, 77, 128

W
Waring, Fred, 103, 121
Webster, Margaret, 129–130
Westminster Choir College, 26–27, 87, 132
White, John Simon, 130–131
Wilcox, John C., 75, 131
Williamson, Dr. John Finley, 25–28, 131–132

Listen, and view, Herbert Beattie on YouTube:

Herbert Beattie Opera Bass

https://youtu.be/PS5SBcRBX7E

About the Type

NOTES BELOW THE STAFF

is set in *Adobe Minion Pro*.

Minion is an old style serif typeface inspired by letters used during the late Renaissance-era. It was designed in 1990 by Robert Slimbach for Adobe Systems. It has proven to be a popular and adaptive type, used for everything from Stieg Larsson's Millennium Trilogy to other languages including Arabic, Cyrillic, Hebrew, Thai, and Song (Chinese). Minion is noted for its versatility, warmth and balance, making it one of the most readable and widely-used fonts available today.

Editing: Lauren Arnest
Typesetting: Don Kallaus
Indexing: Steve Adams

www.ingramcontent.com/pod-product-compliance
Lightning Source LLC
Chambersburg PA
CBHW061604110426
42742CB00039B/2794